In a world of ever increasing uncertainty, fear, and separation, we drown in conflicts. The conflicts take root not in our weaknesses but in our strengths. In this amazing book we learn how to integrate our competing strengths to co-create the world for which we all yearn. It is a must read.

— Robert Quinn, Professor Emeritus, Ross School of Business, University of Michigan

We live in a world of disruption that makes us either turn backwards by closing our mind, heart, and will (i.e. amplifying ignorance, hate, fear) or leaning forward through opening our mind, heart, and will (i.e. cultivating curiosity, compassion, courage). Which of these two pathways we embody is a question of our intention and our capacity. This book tells you how to develop the capacity for the second path. How to co-create as an individual, as a team, and as an organization. Essential reading for change makers and forward thinking organizations.

— Otto Scharmer, author of Theory U

We are at a period in our collective history where the anticipated changes now emerge as realities that consist of complex and systemic challenges. We need to work together to achieve the seismic shift that can catapult us into a new economic order, which is more social, lean, integrated and circular. The book offers a concrete pathway to achieve the 2030 Agenda for Sustainable Development through much required co-creation. Read the book and be inspired.

— Lise Kingo, Executive Director, United Nations Global Impact

For all leaders – current and future – this book provides an invaluable roadmap. It explains the process of collaboration in a structured way, and shows through a series of practical exercises how leaders can become change makers.

— Paul Polman, Chief Executive Officer, Unilever plc

In times of transformation, the world certainly needs change makers charged with superpowers and Katrin Muff's innovative approach to co-creation has given her invaluable insights into how to cultivate them. An essential and highly readable book.

— Kate Raworth, Doughnut Economics

Five Superpowers for Co-Creators

This groundbreaking and timely book provides change makers, organizations and facilitators with practical tools to initiate and conduct multi-stakeholder co-creation processes. Such processes are of critical importance in times of rapid change, where mega trends and grand challenges influence the market dynamics of business in entirely new ways. The book provides a concrete pathway for business to become future-ready by building capacity to work outside its traditional boundaries.

The book unfolds the shift of multi-stakeholder teams from a state of competition to a state of collaboration, addressing the inner and outer dimensions of such a change. The five superpowers identified in the book are: (1) the genuine engagement of individuals, (2) collective solutions of groups, (3) transformative spaces created by facilitators, (4) the building blocks of co-creation, and (5) an effective strategy process for organizations. The book explores the challenges to achieve each of these superpowers. It also shares the stories of "heroes of transformation" and explores what have been the reasons for their success.

The Sustainable Development Goals (SDGs), the grand challenges, the future of work . . . call it what you want, the future is here and organizations, change makers and facilitators need nothing less than these superpowers to collaborate with other players to solve these wicked problems.

Katrin Muff is a thought leader, consultant and facilitator in the transformative space of sustainability and responsibility. From 2008 to 2018, she has helped shape Business School Lausanne, first as Dean and later as Professor in Business Sustainability & Responsibility. Prior to this, she worked as a strategist for Alcoa in Europe, the U.S. and Russia and for P&G in the Netherlands. She holds a PhD from Exeter University, an MBA from BSL and is a certified coach.

This book is ideal for:

- Experienced and aspiring change makers who seek to maximize their positive impact organizational leaders of any kind who want to re-orient, align or transform the core competencies of their organization towards a positive force for society and the world and hence ensuring its survival in a VUCA world;
- Teachers in leadership, business development, organizational change & development, strategy, and business sustainability, who need concrete material for class sessions on the many dimensions of bringing about positive change with stakeholders;
- Facilitators of change who wish to scale their transformational effectiveness with new process and development insights, particularly in the context of hosting multi-stakeholder processes.

You can use this guide as a change maker or organizational leaders, and as a learning tool for aspiring change makers. Each chapter includes reflection questions and exercises as well as further readings and can be used separately either for self-study or in a formal learning context. It is ideal for flipped classroom learning.

Five Superpowers for Co-Creators

How change makers and business can achieve the Sustainable Development Goals

Katrin Muff

Routledge
Taylor & Francis Group
LONDON AND NEW YORK

LiFT Leadership for Transition

Co-funded by the
Erasmus+ Programme
of the European Union

First published 2019
by Routledge
2 Park Square, Milton Park, Abingdon, Oxon OX14 4RN

and by Routledge
711 Third Avenue, New York, NY 10017

Routledge is an imprint of the Taylor & Francis Group, an informa business

British Library Cataloguing-in-Publication Data
A catalogue record for this book is available from the British
Library

Library of Congress Cataloging-in-Publication Data
Names: Muff, Katrin, author.
Title: Secrets, steps and superpowers of co-creation : a guide to
    achieve the sdgs for change makers and organizations alike / by
    Katrin Muff.
Description: First Edition. | New York : Routledge, 2019. | Includes
    bibliographical references and index.
Identifiers: LCCN 2018029323 | ISBN 9781138608412 (hardback) |
    ISBN 9781138608429 (pbk.) | ISBN 9780429466540 (ebook)
Subjects: LCSH: Group problem solving. | Organizational change. |
    International cooperation.
Classification: LCC HD30.29 .M84 2019 | DDC 658.4/036—dc23
LC record available at https://lccn.loc.gov/2018029323

ISBN: 978-1-138-60841-2 (hbk)
ISBN: 978-1-138-60842-9 (pbk)
ISBN: 978-0-429-46654-0 (ebk)

Typeset in Garamond
by Apex CoVantage, LLC

Co-funded by the EU in connection with a Leadership for
Transition project (LiFT)

Contents

Figures

Tables

Acknowledgments

This book stands on the shoulders of giants.

In particular on those of my fellow authors of the Collaboratory book to which this book is a sequel. Anders Aspling, Jackie Bagnall, Jannickette Blainey, Eddie Blass, Anthony Buono, Bill Burck, Mark Drewell, Thomas Dyllick, Patrick Frick, Ronald Fry, Louie Gardiner, Jonas Haertle, Zaid Hassan, Peter Hayward, Stephen Hickman, Adame Kahane, Claire Maxwell, Philip Mirvis, John North, Caroline Rennie, Svenja Rüger, Otto Scharmer, Gregoire Serikoff, Paul Shrivastava, and Aaron Williamson.

It builds on the unwavering support, personal examples, and critical reflection of my partners in facilitation and in life: Christiane Seuhs-Schoeller, Claudia Kraenefuss, Chris Laszlo, Otto Scharmer, J. B. Kassarjian, Carlo Giardinetti, Thomas Dyllick, Caroline Rennie, Sue Muff-Sprenger, Berit Ann Roos, Josef Muff, Swami Brahmdev, Elizabeth Wirsching, Rosemarie Dyllick-Brenzinger, John North, Mark Drewell, Marielle Heijtjes, Derick de Jongh, John Cimino, Jonathan Gosling, Aileen Ionescu-Somers, Jonathan Reims, Elke Fein, Chris Taylor, Robert Quinn, Denitsa Marinova, and Barbara Dubach. Thank you for sharing good and bad moments, for your patience, the space to be silent, and in particular for your capacity to listen and to hear.

I am indebted also to the precious Collaboratory experiences and the uncountable change makers whose paths I was lucky to cross and whose stories have enriched this book.

Deep gratitude to Agnieszka Kapalka, my research sparring partner at Business School Lausanne and in a variety of projects of the Mission Possible Foundation for her unwavering support, encouragement, inspiration, and practical advice in the final revision of the book. Big thanks also to John Peters for his publishing advice and to Rebecca Mash and Judith Lorton for their invaluable editorial support at Routledge Publishing. Thank you David Kibbe for your creative input for the book cover design.

Thank you also to my partners at the European research initiative Leadership for transition, short LiFT, and at Business School Lausanne for having granted me the space and time to put pen to paper, or better fingers to keyboard, and to face the challenge of finding words for what has not been said before.

Katrin Muff, Lausanne in August 2018

Foreword by Paul Polman: co-creation in the era of the SDGs

Over the last 50 years the world has witnessed the greatest economic expansion of all time. Average per capita incomes have trebled and the global economic has increased six-fold in GDP terms. Many have benefitted. More than a billion, for example, have been lifted out of poverty – and huge social improvements and technological progress have enhanced the lives and well-being of millions more.

Yet, for all this, our current model of development is deeply flawed. Rapid economic expansion has come at a price. Rising inequality, weakening job security, and runaway climate change are among factors contributing to growing sense of unease and disaffection. According to one study, less than one in five Americans aged between 18 and 29 now identify themselves as "capitalists."

The truth is the current model is not sustainable, on any level. We need to transform the way we consume so we can live within our planetary boundaries, improve governance to ensure transparency, and accelerate the transition to a just and decarbonized economy.

The good news is that we have an agreed vision of the world we want. The UN Sustainable Development Goals (SDGs) – all 17 of them – and the Paris Climate Change agreement provide a shared roadmap to together build a world that is inclusive, fair, sustainable, stable, and prosperous. And they were agreed by all the nations of the world.

The SDGs have also been described as the world's "business plan." The Business & Sustainable Development Commission has calculated that implementing the SDGs could unlock more than $12 trillion of commercial opportunities across key economic systems, with the potential to create up to 380 million jobs by 2030. No wonder an increasing number of companies are embedding the SDGs into their business strategies.

The brilliance of the SDGs is how closely they are interlinked and SDG 17 – Partnership for the Goals – underscores the value of partnership and collaboration to deliver the systemic shifts we require to achieve these ambitious goals.

The scale and magnitude of the changes we face are too big for any one organization, or even one nation, to deal with alone. Meeting the SDGs will require transformative partnerships – governments, businesses, NGOs, universities – all working together to develop solutions and bring about systemic shifts.

We see some of these partnerships beginning to form – in tackling issues like tropical deforestation for example. By bringing suppliers, manufacturers, customers, and policy-makers together – under the aegis of the Tropical Forest Alliance – we are at last making progress in tackling one of the biggest contributors to global warming, while also helping to secure the future livelihoods of thousands of small hold farmers.

Five Superpowers for Co-Creators provides insights into how such partnerships can work. The book uncovers important insights regarding the process offering building blocks of co-creation, as well as how to overcome conflicts and tensions at the individual and group levels – offering a concrete tool for facilitators. It shows that change makers are everywhere and invites them to contribute to much needed co-created partnerships.

These kind of partnerships are borne of leadership, courageous and unselfish leadership. To succeed they will require a new generation of leaders: men and women driven by a different set of ideals, with moral conviction, favoring harder rights over easier wrongs and willing to do everything in their power to help the world implement the SDGs.

For all leaders – current and future – this book provides an invaluable roadmap. It explains the process of collaboration in a structured way, and shows through a series of practical exercises how leaders can become change makers and embed purpose at the heart of their organization, and work in partnerships with a range of stakeholders to deliver that purpose.

To accelerate the implementation of the SDGs, we need new thinking and this book will guide the next generation of change makers to understand how to drive effective change and to deliver improved societal outcomes. It will help guide those leaders, in whose hands our future lies.

Paul Polman, Geneva in May 2018

Introduction

The issues we face are so big and the targets are so challenging that we cannot do it alone. When you look at any issue, such as food or water scarcity, it is very clear that no individual institution, government or company can provide the solution.
—Paul Polman, CEO of Unilever

We live in the era of the UN Sustainable Development Goals (SDGs). From 2015 to 2030, these 17 global goals seek to unite the global change movements to reach that dream of all of us living well on one planet. And yet, the challenges with the SDGs are neither self-evident nor uncontested and translation work is required to ensure their relevance in every nation and business context. After a few years, priorities start to emerge and engaged citizens shift gear. Business has acknowledged their importance, yet still sits on the fence. Are the SDGs yet one more regulatory ticking-box requirement and a further nuisance to communicate to concerned consumers, or are they really the key to unlock the billion dollars' worth of new business opportunities organizations like the World Economic Forum, the United Nations Global Compact, and the WBCSD claim? If anything, the emerging number of tools, frameworks, and consulting methods are creating confusion and frustration for engaged sustainability practitioners in organizations. We all feel challenged!

No single party can comfortably claim to be able to solve our pressing social, environmental, economic, or governance issue alone, as Paul Polman rightly states. And co-creation efforts of the past decades have shown that the complexity of the inter-connected issues as well as the diversity of stakeholders participating in their solution have become overwhelming.

There are tools that provide clarity and are easy to use for organizations who want to include the challenges expressed by the SDGs as core strategic opportunities in their business. You will learn about them in this book so that you can use them. Yet tools without processes are like bicycles without wheels. The frame alone won't get you anywhere! Process breakdown has caused more projects to be abandoned than the use of inappropriate tools. Yet, there is structure to the madness and this book gives you diagnostic tools and helps fix broken or fragile processes.

Tools pretend to be clean and proper, while processes tend to be sticky and messy. Why? Well, they involve people and organizations with different priorities, points of view, and different capacities of dealing with tension. This book gets right into the ugliness of change processes and offers safe passage on the way forward.

Extended experience in leading and facilitating co-creation processes has allowed condensing our insights into concise concepts to make such processes easier. Stories and experiences of failures have contributed equally to this book as successes and transformative moments of ultimate delight. They generate the key realization that has shaped the work behind the superpower section of the book. The causes of conflict, breakdown, and withdrawal are rooted in original strengths that have been overstretched and turned into serious limitations. Finding the way back to the underlying strength that causes the irritation is a first step toward bringing group processes back to functioning. This work can be done at the individual level, at the group level, and at the shared issue level. When we pair two opposing strengths and reinforce both, superpowers emerge. And this is what we need: solutions, steps, and superpowers so that we can master the journey required to address the burning issues our society and the planet are facing in these coming decades.

This book is the sequel to "the Collaboratory" book that I edited and co-wrote with 29 fellow co-authors in an attempt to clarify the roots of co-creative processes, their application in various sectors, and to help facilitators create their own processes. In this sequel, the focus is on enabling change in service of the common good. We look at how to embrace change as individuals, as groups, and as facilitators of co-creation processes for change makers and organizations, so that multi-stakeholder groups can successfully achieve the positive impact they seek.

The five superpowers for co-creators, both as individuals change makers and for business, are

- Superpower #1: genuine engagement of individuals
- Superpower #2: collective solutions generated by groups
- Superpower #3: transformative spaces created by facilitators
- Superpower #4: building blocks of co-creation for change makers
- Superpower #5: positive-impact tool for organizations.

Book overview

Part I of the book frames the context of change. It considers the capacity of business to disrupt society. Increasingly, we also witness the risks of how society disrupts business. For one, social media has changed the way the public opinion is formed and how quickly a new tipping point can be reached that changes the game overnight. The connections of an individual, society, and organizations has also shifted and has become more obvious and complex. We explore the three interconnections, which are also called the levels of the I, the We, and the All-of-us.

The circle model allows framing these interconnections in the context of our inner and outer worlds and suggests that when individuals meet to solve a societal issue representing either their project or their organization, transformation is possible through connected shifts at all three levels. The Collaboratory process is an established way to create and hold the space for such transformation and here we explore how we can use it to scale change. Shifting from a competitive to a collaborative state is key when attempting such a transformation.

Such a shift involves a group of stakeholders to become issue rather than tribe oriented, to embrace rather than reject differences, to move beyond competing values to co-creating value, and to feel connected within themselves, to others in the project, and the cause. Collaboratory experiences provide some insights to achieve these shifts. Becoming open to a new way of solving a problem, showing up differently, and engaging in a new way of listening. The facilitator is instrumental in creating a space for this.

Part II includes three chapters that outline pathways to integrating related polar strengths into superpowers at three levels to enable a state of collaboration:

- Genuine engagement at the individual level is achieved by combining strength pairs into three superpowers defined as Appreciative, Alliance, and Support.
- Collective solutions at the group level can be achieved by integrating strength polarities and achieving the following superpowers: Deep Search, Collaboration and Mastery.
- Transformative spaces at the shared issue level of the issue can be attributed to the three superpowers of Awareness, Coherence, and Resonance. Each of these is the result of having transformed an underlying strength polarity.

Part III focuses on the true heroes of transformation: the individual change maker. We meet six such change makers in unlikely spaces and professions. We study their individual issues as a starting base to map journeys of development and growth. We discover how each of them contributes in their own way to a multi-stakeholder process, illustrating the diversity of contributions to make a transformation possible. There is no one way.

The initiator of a project and the facilitator hold a special place in co-creation processes. We look in detail at their challenges along each of the nine building blocks of a successful multi-stakeholder co-creation process. We discuss the superpowers of the nine process building blocks and explore each of these. Not every co-creation process needs all of these; however, it is useful to be aware of the small and the large innovation cycle that are likely to be required when new ideas need to be developed and implemented. The SDGX innovation process is used to illustrate a typical Collaboratory day and shows how a company can translate the Sustainable Development Goals (SDGs) into new long-term business opportunities.

Measuring progress in such complex multi-level processes is useful in many ways. The initiator and facilitator can use it to gauge the overall process and potential blind spots that prevents advancement. The 45 dimensions of the responsible leadership grid allow mapping the current state of development in each of the nine building blocks across knowledge, skills, and competencies. The seven change agents illustrate the journey of change with personal stories. As an example, the Impact Leadership Program shows how co-creative processes can be connected with educational offers to develop future-capable leaders while working on strategic sustainability projects for companies.

Part IV focuses on how to translate the building blocks to organizational initiatives to work with stakeholders on implementing sustainability, or the SDGs, into their strategy. It proposes a simplified process that builds on the small innovation cycle as an organizational superpower. It outlines options for both entrepreneurial and intrapreneurial change makers using flexible processes depending on the situation. Taking into account culture, governance, decision-making processes, and status in the sustainability journey of an organization is important, as they influence the starting point of a co-creation process.

The **conclusion** brings together the five superpowers across the individual, the group and the facilitated levels as well as for change makers and for organizations. The chapter highlights how the superpowers interplay so that any change makers, organizations and facilitator has a solid support in their positive impact journey.

Glossary of terms

As in any field, there is lingo in co-creation and change process work. This here should help:

Action Research	A reflective process of progressive problem solving led by individuals working with others in teams or as part of a "community of practice," and representing a variety of evaluative, investigative, and analytical research methods designed to diagnose problems.
Appreciative Inquiry	Both a philosophical approach to organizational change and a concrete change management approach that focuses on identifying what is working well, analyzing why it is working well, and then doing more of it.
Business-as-usual (BAU)	Normal conduct of business in current dominant paradigm of short-term profit maximization for the principle benefit of its shareholders.
Business Sustainability Today	A visual platform with the purpose of showcasing advanced sustainability organizations and their best practices in form of short, professional videos. Business Sustainability Today website: https://sustainability-today.com
Business Sustainability Typology (BST)	A framework that offers a practical approach to evaluate different levels of integration of sustainability in business. This typology ranges from Business Sustainability 1.0 (Refined Shareholder Value Management) to Business Sustainability 2.0 (Managing for the Triple Bottom Line) and to Business Sustainability 3.0 (True Sustainability). *See the animated explainer video*: www.youtube.com/watch?v=AEFqUh4PMmI&feature=youtu.be *Read the original paper*: Dyllick, T., Muff, K. (2016): *Clarifying the Meaning of Sustainable Business: Introducing a Typology from Business-as-Usual to True Business Sustainability*. Organization & Environment. Vol. 29, No. 2, 2016, 156–174.

Collaboratory	A co-creative, open-space engagement process for hosting multi-stakeholder conversations to generate solutions to complex problems. The Collaboratory empowers citizens to jointly question, discuss, and construct new ideas and approaches to resolving sustainability challenges on a local, regional, and global level. *See the explainer video*: www.youtube.com/watch?v=SYCZ4Ep-oss *Read the Collaboratory handbook*: The Collaboratory: A co-creative stakeholder engagement process for solving complex problems, Sheffield: Greenleaf Publishing, 2004, Edited by Katrin Muff
Competency Assessment of Responsible Leadership (CARL)	An online test which builds a profile around 45 Responsible Leadership (RL) competencies and three domains of action (knowing, doing, being). The CARL was developed by a group of Thought Leaders committed to the development of Responsible Leadership. *See the explainer video*: www.youtube.com/watch?v=tlbbsqX9bVs *Visit the CARL website*: https://carl2030.org/ *Take the CARL free online test*: https://carl2030.org/survey/
Competing Values Framework	A conceptual model for diagnosing and changing organizational culture, developed by Quin and Cameron. The Organizational Culture Assessment Instrument (OCAI) is an online test that allows to assess the organizational culture. *See the explainer video*: www.youtube.com/watch?v=45veR-Se-rI *Visit the OCAI website*: www.ocai-online.com/ *Read the original paper*: Cameron, K. S. & Quinn, R. E. (2005). *Diagnosing and changing organizational culture: Based on the competing values framework*, John Wiley & Sons.
Dialogic Organizational Development (DOD)	A concept developed by Bushe and Marshak that assumes that organizational change results from "changing the conversations" that shape behavior of people. DOD emphasizes discourse, emergence, and generativity to foster and accelerate change in organizations. Generativity creates change by offering people new images that allow them to see old things in new ways.

Emergence creates change by disrupting stable patterns and creating opportunities for new thoughts. Discourse creates change by altering the stories and symbols people use to make meaning of themselves and the situation they are in.
See the explainer video:
www.youtube.com/watch?v=myyj15AfH3Q
Visit the dialogicod.net website that provides free resources and links to tools and articles on DOD:
www.dialogicod.net

Dynamic Facilitation	A facilitation style that follows the energy of the group without constraining that energy to agenda or exercises.
Facilitator	A person who facilitates stakeholder co-creation or innovation sessions on request of the "owner" of the co-creation process. The "owner" may request further facilitation support in other building blocks of the process.
Fishbowl	A methodology for hosting large group dialogues. Within this method, four to five participants are selected to discuss the topic in an inner circle (fishbowl). The audience (remaining participants) are placed in concentric circles outside the fishbowl.
Focused Reporting	A project that promotes comprehensive, credible, and relevant sustainability reporting of Swiss companies. *Visit the Focused Reporting website*: www.focusedreporting.ch
GAPFRAME	A framework that translates the Sustainable Development Goals (SDGs) 2030 into nationally relevant issues. The framework is used as a strategic business tool to identify long-term business opportunities and as an educational tool to sensitize students to relevant sustainability issues. *See the explainer video*: www.youtube.com/watch?v=MNXhkv3-UfI *Visit the GAPFRAME website*: http://gapframe.org
GRIPS	Innovation process that provides guidance and support in co-creation of new strategic business opportunities. The SDGX innovation process builds on the Sustainable Development Goals (SDGs) and the Business Sustainability Typology (BST) and enables organizations to reflect and focus on long-term solutions creating a net-positive impact for all.

	See the explainer video: www.youtube.com/watch?time_continue=153&v=Gzi LI9Xz1WY *Visit the SDGXCHANGE platform to learn more about the GRIPS*: https://sdgx.org
Holacracy	A customizable self-management practice for running purpose-driven and responsive organizations. This method supports agile organizational structure, autonomous teams, and decentralized management and organizational governance. *See the explainer video*: www.youtube.com/watch?time_continue=11&v=YBM H4HLilSE *Visit the Holacracy website*: www.holacracy.org
Impact Leadership Program (ILP)	A program that aims at development of future-relevant leadership competencies, helping organizations to sustain in the *volatile*, *uncertain*, *complex*, and *ambiguous* (VUCA) world. *See the description of the Impact Leadership Program*: https://www.katrinmuff.com
Initiator	The "owner" of the innovation process.
Open Space Technology	A methodology for hosting large group dialogues. It includes a way for hosting conferences, symposiums, and community summit events that are focused on a specific task but have no initial formal agenda beyond the overall purpose or theme.
Outside-in perspective	The outside-in business perspective draws attention to society and sustainability challenges, as opposite to the *inside-out perspective* that has a strong focus on the business and profit. *See the explainer video*: www.youtube.com/watch?v=AEFqUh4PMmI
Paris Climate Agreement	Agreement adopted in 2015 by the United Nations that aims to respond to the global climate change by keeping a global temperature rise this century below 2 degrees Celsius above pre-industrial levels. Additionally, the agreement aims to strengthen the ability of countries to deal with the impacts of climate change. *Visit the United Nations website*: http://unfccc.int/paris_agreement/items/9485.php

Pilot	A confirmed proof of concept tested with clients and accompanied with a business plan as an outcome of a prototype process.
Prototype	The conceptual output from an ideation session that is then further developed and advanced into initial proof of concept.
Reporting Matters	Reporting methodology developed by the World Business Council for Sustainable Development (WBCSD) in order to improve the effectiveness of non-financial corporate reporting. *Visit the WBCSD website*: www.wbcsd.org/Projects/Reporting/Reporting-matters
RepRisk reports	Reports providing an in-depth look at an individual company's environment, social, and governance (ESG) risk exposure. *Visit the RepRisk website*: www.reprisk.com
SPRINT	A five-day process for answering critical business questions through design, prototyping, and testing new ideas with customers.
Superpower	A superpower is a higher level performance that is achieved when two opposing strengths are mastered.
Sustainable Development Goals (SDGs)	A set of 17 global goals adopted in 2015 by the United Nations with the aim to end poverty, protect the planet and ensure prosperity for all. *See the explainer video*: https://vimeo.com/151435077 *See the United Nations website*: www.un.org/sustainabledevelopment/sustainable-development-goals/
Theory U	A change management method that describes the process of becoming a person, group, or organization which develops co-creative space where everyone works with an open mind, open heart, and open will. This fosters "presencing" conversations in which unexpected creative ideas pop-up. *Visit the Presencing Institute website*: www.presencing.
Visioning exercise	An exercise run during a co-creation or ideation session, where participants are guided into a future space to experience (feel, smell, hear, sense, taste) a world where the issue is resolved. At the end of the exercise, participants

	report what they have experienced in order to create a shared vision which is the source of inspiration for future solutions to be developed. *Visit the Presencing Institute website*: www.presencing.org
VUCA	The VUCA acronym is an abbreviation of *Volatility, Uncertainty, Complexity,* and *Ambiguity*. The VUCA term was introduced by the U.S. Army War College to describe more a volatile, uncertain, complex, and ambiguous world. Today, the VUCA term is commonly used in a wide range of organizations, mainly in the strategic leadership domain.
WBCSD	The World Business Council for Sustainable Development (WBCSD) is a global organization of over 200 leading businesses working together to accelerate the transition to a sustainable world. *Visit the WBCSD website*: www.wbcsd.org
World Café	A methodology for hosting large group dialogues. It is a structured conversational process in which groups of people discuss a topic at several tables, switching tables periodically and getting introduced to the discussions being previously held.

Speed-reading in less than 50 sentences

Chapter I The interconnection of society, organizations, and individuals

- Society has an impact on business and the SDGs frame these challenges as opportunities.
- Business has an impact on society
- People have an impact on business. And business has an impact on people.
- Change makers are at the heart of small groups of people that change the world.
- Synching our inner world with the outer world is a basis for transformation.
- When individuals and organizations work on societal issues, transformative change happens.
- Multi-stakeholder co-creation is dependent on the creation of a shared issue.
- The introspective capacity of stakeholders defines the potential of change.
- The facilitator's role is central to creating and holding the space for stakeholder co-creation.
- Practice and increase your self-regulation capacity as you continue.

Chapter 2 The dynamics of stakeholder transformation

- Complex problems require appropriate practices to achieve the desired solutions.
- Stakeholders are challenged to achieve a mindset shift from competition to cooperation.
- When operating in a state of competition, the space is filled with inner and outer chatter.
- When operating in a state of cooperation, the space is filled with emerging resonance.
- When stakeholders find new ways to work together, co-creation suddenly works.

- They start to show up differently and be present more authentically.
- New ways of listening open the space for co-creating new value and benefits.
- These spaces are facilitated in a way to create connection among previous strangers.
- Effective co-creation requires an inner and outer development of first competencies and then superpowers.

Chapter 3 Superpower #1 – genuine engagement of individuals

- Overcoming the need to be right and to judge others is a challenge for individuals.
- Genuine Engagement develops when participants turn their strengths into superpowers.
- Appreciation results from being critical and positive, overcoming self-righteous judgment.
- Alliance happens when an inclusive influencer stops being opinionated or unprincipled.
- Support comes from being open and caring, resisting the temptation to be distant and impatient.
- Appreciation, Alliance, and Support are superpowers for Genuine Engagement.

Chapter 4 Superpower #2 – collective solutions of groups

- Finding the right balance between analyzing the problem versus visioning is a group challenge.
- Collective Solutions unfold when the participating groups embrace their superpowers.
- A deep search arises from analysis and vision, letting go of the problem and the dream.
- Collaboration results from prototyping, multiplicity beyond single interest and quick solutions.
- Mastery combines efficacy with sharing, overcoming a need for protection or specialization.
- Deep search, Collaboration, and Mastery are the superpowers for Collective Solutions.

Chapter 5 Superpower #3 – transformative spaces of facilitators

- The challenge in holding the space for a shared issue is being too strict or lost in facilitation.

- Transformative spaces emerge when the common space of a shared issue is full of superpowers.
- Awareness enables an adaptive structure that is neither too strict nor disconnected.
- Coherence is the ideal of breakthrough and harmony, avoiding breakdown and dissonance.
- Resonance occurs in moments of stillness and connection, overcoming agitation and fragmentation.
- Awareness, Coherence and Resonance are superpowers for transformative spaces.

Chapter 6 The different types and roles of change makers

- There is a change maker either in you or near you; they all greatly care for the world.
- Company leaders struggle to find answers for the emerging challenges of a fast-changing world.
- Lack of clarity about the issue results in lack of clarity of the process and the roles of those involved.
- Diversity among participants is key for co-creation, and a source of disagreement and creativity.
- Light that fire and have that conversation of achieving positive impact with a change maker near you!
- A great process can channel the potential of emerging contributors into a small group of change makers!

Chapter 7 Superpower #4 – the building blocks of co-creation

- Clarifying expectations of all participants, again and again, is a key for successful collaboration.
- A facilitator allows the initiator to focus on the ideas and the people, rather than the process.
- There are two innovations in co-creation: a small cycle of rapid prototyping and a larger overall process.
- The co-creation sessions are the heart of process and the moment where magic is orchestrated.
- The nine different building blocks of a co-creation process cover the initiator, co-creation events, and scaling.
- Understanding the key activities in each of the building blocks provides clarity in process design.

Chapter 8 Measuring progress in co-creation

- Each participant and change maker is challenged to develop new competencies when working co-creatively.

- Superpower elements show similarities with process competencies but can't (yet) serve to measure progress.
- Competencies of responsible leadership can serve as a frame for assessing the development of participants.
- Core competencies an initiator is challenged to develop in each of the building blocks of co-creation.
- Core competencies any participants can further develop during a co-creation process.
- Opportunities for competencies development for a facilitator along the co-creation process.
- The status and development of individual competencies is the biggest blind spot of social change projects.

Chapter 9 Superpower #5 – The positive-impact tool of organizations

- For your tailor-made co-creation and change process, play with the building blocks.
- Organizations need processes that work internally and connect with relevant players externally.
- When organizations drive co-creation processes with a tight set of practical tools and processes.
- The SDGX innovation process shows how the co-creation building blocks work with corporate strategy.
- Solving pressing societal issues challenges the strategic thinking processes of organizations.
- Embedding sustainability opportunities into your strategy will change your organization and its governance.
- Dare to stumble into stillness, void of inner and outer chatter, and sense the resonance of co-creation.

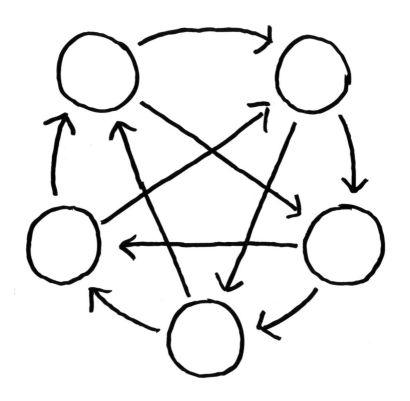

Part I

The dynamics of change

Achieving change is complex in a world where society impacts business, business impacts society, and business and people impact and influence each other. In these times of rapid change and increasing complexity among inter-connected issues, business is challenged to become better in managing beyond its boundaries.

Chapter 1 *highlights the disruptive effect of society on business and vice versa, and the connection between an individual and an organization. These interconnections are explored using the circle model, which connects the inner world with the outer world. It opens the space of emerging transformation that occurs when personal, organizational, and societal development coincide in a multistakeholder co-creation (or Collaboratory) process. These three dimensions of the I, We, and All-of-us provide the foundation of multi-stakeholder collaboration.*

Chapter 2 *demonstrates how these three dimensions play in multi-stakeholder collaborations, and how they enable the shift from a state of competition to a state of collaboration. These two states are explored in-depth and serve to frame the challenges of making stakeholder processes successful. Key insights from fellow facilitators introduce first ideas to understand these challenges by integrating competing strength polarities at the level of the individual, the group, and the shared issue.*

If there was one image that could summarize Part I, it would be Figure I.1 that illustrates both states that exist when different parties work together: that of competition and that of co-creation. It shows that the journey from one to the other is about dealing with differences differently. That values can connect rather than divide and that listening to what is going on inside is an important anchor and resource for co-creation, possibly allowing that difficult shift to put an issue ahead of one's "tribe." In a time where business impacts people, and people impact business, where the next scandal is only an effective social media campaign away and where transparency is no longer a luxury but a pre-condition, the demands on the individual, each of us, are tremendous. We can no longer afford to be switched off or distracted while auto-piloting through life. Every day offers multiple challenge that will define how we are perceived by others, be it a casual bystander or an important business partner. The journey of personal development toward becoming increasingly responsible in the way we lead our life is directly coupled with the journey of organizational development that demands a net positive contribution to society and the world. As individuals, we are familiar with these inner and outer worlds and we all navigate them more or less attentively. We have found that co-creation projects with other stakeholders are outstanding moments in time where we can bring in both the best of ourselves as well as the best our organizations have to offer, and this alignment toward a higher goal has transformative powers that will continue to change the world. And this is, after all, what this book is dedicated to.

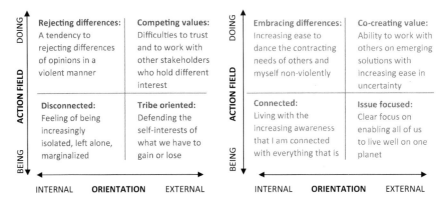

Figure 1.1 The transition from a state of competition (left) to a state of co-creation (right)

Chapter 1

The interconnection of society, organizations, and individuals

Society has an impact on business and the SDGs frame these challenges as opportunities

The head of one of the oldest Swiss banks sits a last time behind his large oak wooden desk. His hands caress the smooth surface and he takes a deep long breath. Never in a million years would he have imagined that the Geneva-based investment bank that his grandfather founded would be shut down. Thinking of his grandfather made him sit up straighter. He would turn in his grave if he were to live this day.

It is not as if they had done anything wrong. The bank was known for treating its employees very well, providing generous Christmas baskets to all families, offering a generous vacation and pension plan, and in the past decade, they even opened their very own childcare center for their staff. Their inside fitness club with the Olympic pool was the envy of the industry and a rooftop cocktail bar notorious on Friday nights. They had more talent wanting to work for them than they could employ.

Their business has – like many other Swiss banks – consisted of safeguarding the wealth of important people around the world. Kings, princes, heads of state, politicians, and of course the occasional celebrity in film or sport. They carried these secrets with pride and with a barely noticeable smile. There was nothing more honorable than maintaining this secrecy and the banking sector has made Switzerland world-famous for this art. Until the turn of the century, that is. It all started in 2008, when Hervé Falciani, a systems engineer at HSBC, leaked more than 130,000 suspected tax evaders to the ex-French Minister Christine Lagarde. He was indicted in absentia in 2014 by the Swiss government for violating the country's bank secrecy laws, but the eggs were long spilled.

In the course of the past decade, the unthinkable has become acceptable. The Swiss reputation as a trustworthy partner and the ability to hold a secret is tarnished and the bank secrecy is viewed as a haven of illicit money. The public perception has simply flipped and the US persecution of numerous Swiss banks has cost them billions of Swiss Francs in penalties for having helped tax evasion internationally. In late 2016, the Swiss Government has formally signed a series of agreements that represent the end of Swiss bank secrecy step by step in 2017 and 2018. Signing these agreements was important for the integrity and weakened reputation of Switzerland's financial center. A change of perspective of such radical nature that as little as 10 years prior, nobody could have anticipated.

As the seasoned Swiss banker rises from his desk, grabbing his 30-year-old brown leather briefcase, he takes a last look across the river through the bay windows of his office. He was glad to be close enough to retirement not to have to worry about what this change would mean for his career. He was equally disturbed that his son was insisting on a banking career, how could there be any banking in a time where split-second trade gains were the only hope for a halfway decent income?

The end of the Swiss banking secret is one of a number of disruptive changes business is facing because of changing public perception and international pressure on local practices. The example is telling as it concerns questionable practices of a respected highly developed country, not an emerging country with practices that may not yet be up to the scrutiny of international standards. The emission scandal of German carmakers tells a similar story. Common and seemingly shared practices in a developed country suddenly face international scrutiny and crumble in the light of investigation. Companies take heavy financial and reputational hits and struggle to understand how this could have possibly happened. The public perception of what is ethical and what not, changes faster than companies can anticipate. Helped by social media, society has become a disruptive force for business.

These disruptions may be seen as risks or as opportunities – depending on your business model. Here things get interesting. How could you position your organization so that you can benefit from the changing perception, the burning issues in society, and what new business opportunities emerge for you from this? We are now in the SDGs era. A time marked by the significant achievement that happened in September 2015, where 193 countries agreed that the Sustainable Developments Goals (the SDGs) define the global agenda for the coming 15 years. The 17 underlying goals are also referred to as the Agenda 2030 (see Figure 1.1). They set the frame for multi-stakeholder

Figure 1.1 The 17 Sustainable Development Goals defining the global agenda until 2030

Image source: www.un.org/sustainabledevelopment/blog/2015/09/why-should-you-care-about-the-sustainable-development-goals/

engagement of our times. As Paul Polman has said so well, these challenges are too big and too complex to be solved by a single institution, government, or company. Only together do we stand a chance of dealing with these issues.

Business has the choice to take a proactive approach toward these global challenges. Many organizations such as the World Economic Forum (WEF), the United Nations Global Compact (UNGC), or the World Business Council for Sustainable Development (WBCSD) have suggested that these global challenges are truly hidden business opportunities, which are estimated to represent billion dollars of new revenues for business. Figuring out how to adapt current strategy processes to embrace such opportunities is a major challenge for business. Chapter 9 offers a concrete answer to this challenging question, introducing both tools and processes for business to embrace these opportunities. This book focuses on helping change makers in organizations and independent of organizations design a journey for achieving these opportunities.

Business has an impact on society

We have also seen how business has impacted society. There is increasing awareness of what it means for society when business disregards its externalities – the cost that do not bear a price tag but may represent a cost to the environment or to society. Take the unaccounted-for cost of forestry activities in terms of soil degradation, biodiversity loss, forced displacement of native tribes, or dried up rivers creating water security issues. Consider the impact of the fast fashion trend with its human rights issues along the supply chain. The mountains of discarded clothes from the developed world that bury developing countries such as Haiti or Ghana. The unprecedented amount of micro-fiber particles in rivers and oceans because of washing cheap fabrics. The wasted resources of surplus clothes that don't sell and hence are burned by the likes of H&M and their peers. These are examples of negative impact on society because of an opportunistic business opportunity that has changed consumer behavior. There are of course also positive consequences of some business initiatives. The educational offer that is available in otherwise isolated communities because of access to the internet. The ability to share cars, bicycles, or scooters as a result of using existing technology creating new consumer trends that reduce the number of cars purchased and number of kilometers driven. The ability to distribute and sell otherwise unaffordable HIV medication in developing countries through business model innovation that seeks to address a societal issue rather than maximize self-interest. These and many other examples greatly demonstrate the ability of business to impact society. Business has become aware of its responsibility and is adapting. By November 2017, more than 1400 business organizations have started accounting for an internal price of carbon. Many of them have come to understand this as a great driver for innovation and efficiency.

People have an impact on business and business has an impact on people

This interconnection of business and society is one dimension to consider. The other dimension concerns the interconnection of people and business.

Christoph is in his mid-50s and the head of the largest division of a big Swiss company. He is recently divorced and quite invested in the career search of his son. As they finish their weekly game of badminton and relax over some iced tea, he struggles – not for the first time – to connect with how his 22-year-old son sees the world. His son disagrees with his career choice that has landed him on the executive team. He wants to work for a small company, one that its purpose is not profit driven. He doesn't see how the work Christoph does for this big corporation is making any sense for the world; he feels that such may actually contribute to further destroying the world. Christoph feels very differently.

He has dedicated his life to be an authentic responsible leader, and he feels that he makes a key difference in the company with the perspective that he brings in to the executive team. Not that it is always easy! Sometimes, he scratches his head in some of these executive meetings and wonders how he can indeed ensure that he does good for the world while his company is under so much pressure to improve the top and the bottom line of the business. Just the other day, the group CFO told him: "Your sustainability ideas just cost too much and we cannot afford to do more than we already do."

Yet, when Christoph talks with his buddy who oversees Human Resources, they have different conversations. They wonder about how they can retain the new generation that ticks so differently from how they have grown up and who want such different things. Christoph sees no conflict in all of that. He believes that the future generation is exactly what the company needs to bring the kind of innovation power to drive the company forward into the 21st century. He does however get the point that not everybody has what it takes to work on such innovation projects. But that is something his HR colleague would hopefully be able to sort out. As a strategist, he knows there must be a way to bridge the difference of what is right for the common good, what he feels pressured to do for the company, and what is actually right for the company.

On the treadmill at lunchtime, he tries to catch-up with his backlog of reading. He groans as he finishes an interval series and reduces the incline to take a deep breath. Christoph shakes his head about the large pile of new articles and blogs that discuss new tools around the

Sustainable Development Goals, the latest of external pressures placed on corporations. He cannot keep up with all the readings. What he needs are answers, not more questions! How can these ideas to save the world be translated into clear-cut business opportunities? Where are the quick tools and the easy answers? If he cannot see through it, how can he ever expect his colleagues at the executive team to buy into a new strategic approach that re-orients his company around burning issues of the world rather than short-term responses to the latest competitive threat?

This story shows the interconnection of an individual and the organization in which he works. We all have several roles that we embrace in both our personal and professional aspects of life. Finding an internal coherence among these roles is a lifelong adventure. The importance a single person can bring to an organization has never been doubted. Paul Polman, current CEO of Unilever, is an example for the degree of change a single person in the right position of a multinational organization can accomplish. He hits far above his weight – both in terms of how he is guiding his organization around a grounded sustainability and responsibility vision, and how he has stepped up in expression of his opinion in the public domain. He is using the role power as CEO to embed his values'-based beliefs of the role of business in society. He is inviting and challenging other businesses to do the same. When his son interviews him about his CEO role, he says that what is important to him is that he is in a role where he can express his fullest potential and that is what he invites his son to seek as well. Whatever role that may be. Indeed, expressing our fullest potential, wherever we are, is what defines a responsible leadership. In the 21st century, leaders are no longer those few who formally lead, but the many that make important decisions, in whatever position they hold, in whatever in which organization they work. As such, anybody in any role has significant potential to contribute to the change for which we are looking and to which this book is dedicated.

Change makers are at the heart of small groups of people that change the world

There are different types of change makers and this book caters to as many of them as possible. There are those with a great desire to contribute to a better world, without knowing exactly how and with whom. They want to learn, gain more experience, and add new competencies to solve burning issues with which they are either directly concerned or that they know about. There are those who have possibly a preset opinion of how things should be and who would ensure that new innovations don't create more problems, but better solutions. Then there are those who have a perfect solution for just about any problem. These people either have a process that can work for any problem and will seek for problems that they can help solve. They are an incredible asset for any change-making process. There are those who are self-employed, those who work in small business, multinationals, universities, and business schools, those who either have founded an NGO or are employed by one. There are those open for change and those challenged by it. Those far advanced in their own personal development and those at the brink of discovery. It is this colorful mix of people with their different stances and motivations that are – each in their own way – contributing to change the world. And those few is all we really need!

> **Never doubt that a small group of thoughtful, committed citizens can change the world; indeed, it's the only thing that ever has.**
> Margaret Mead

Margaret Mead has inspired many of us to attempt change. This book takes this quote as an ingoing true assumption and provides concrete pathways for realizing this promise. As such, it provides an answer to the challenging question of how societal change can be created by a small group of individuals. The time for such an answer has never been more right than now. The answer includes a solid understanding of the societal, the organizational, and the individual interconnections in finding new ways of collaborating across existing boundaries. The SDGs and the global agenda provide a useful framework for change makers to focus and prioritize their actions and projects. Translation tools such as the GAPFRAME (www.gapframe.org) allow a quick overview of what the burning priorities are of more than 150 countries. So if you are a change maker, before launching your next project, verify your own agenda in the context of what the world needs most. Being able to find a match between what matters to you and what is most needed in the world is incredibly important if you care about maximizing your positive impact.

Synching our inner world with the outer world is a basis for transformation

These interconnections are critical when we want to understand how change happens. The Circle Model (Figure 1.2) represents the interconnection of what happens in the "outer" and the "inner" worlds. While we are busy in our corporate jobs, we focus on our contribution in the world: contributing in roles to enable business to become truly sustainable. This connects

Figure 1.2 The Circle Model showing the interconnection of Personal and Organizational Development (Muff 2016)

to the previous examples and what is here called the "outer world." At the same time, there is an "inner world" to all of us that is more or less tended. In this space, we reflect about our ability to act based on our values and with increasing integration of what we learn, we develop toward responsible leaders. A responsible leader in this context is understood as anybody who assumes an active responsibility for the impact they have in the world through the multiple roles they occupy in all aspects of life. The circle model suggests an emerging transformation that is ongoing in the continuous interaction between our inner and outer worlds in our life. As the alignment of our activities in the outer world and our perception of our inner world increases, the values'-based inner drive and the organizational actualized desire to contribute positively to the world merge into a virtuous circle.

The empty center in the middle of the circle model is the imaginary space or moment where transformative magic happens. In our **Collaboratory** action and research activities, we have paid particular attention to observe this phenomenon. We have noticed that individuals, who both represent an organization in a Collaboratory and personally care about the issue discussed, undergo a deep change during a Collaboratory process. They emerge profoundly more integrated in who they are with renewed clarity of their purpose in the world and the significance of their engagement in their organization. In a group, there is something larger at play than when individuals work on themselves and improve, for example, their mindfulness. Otto Scharmer refers to it as consciousness and the one independent variable that can facilitate a change in reducing the sense of separation of body and mind and contribute to personal integration. Space opens up and time slows down. While these extraordinary

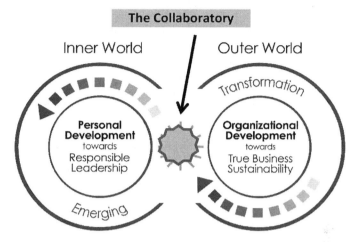

Figure 1.3 The Circle Model with the Collaboratory illustrating the magic space of transformation

moments don't need to be attained the entire time, it is in such moments that the transformation shifts happen. This book builds on these insights and investigates how to accelerate and scale such multi-level transformations. Figure 1.3 shows the Collaboratory in this empty space symbolizing its unique place in enabling multi-level transformation.

When individuals and organizations work on societal issues, transformative change happens

Otto Scharmer refers to the phenomenon of multi-stakeholder work as the possibility to access and modify the social field. It is a space of trust that opens up when individuals are able to express themselves with courage and vulnerability, in a space that is held with deep listening and unconditional listening. This social field is the result of mindfulness in a group, palpable in the density of the stillness that can open up. When the depth of the inner space is activated, such a social field becomes what Scharmer calls a generative field in which participants connect to their deepest sources of creativity, both individually and collectively. Another way to express this is to say that people change their habitual thinking from the head to the heart, becoming aware more broadly and accessing a state of presencing. This involves a shift from moving from a third person perspective (they), to a second person perspective (you) to a first person experience (I) and then an integrated experience including all three perspectives. This book addresses the challenges at the individual, the group, and the shared issue level as interrelated elements of success. Scharmer describes this as the boundary of the self and the other collapsing resulting in a de-centering of self.

Research on the topic of Global Responsibility calls these spaces the I, We, All-of-us levels of responsibility. The I-space relates to the individual level of development, the space where you and I can act as individuals. In this book, this is the individual level of multi-stakeholder processes. The We-space describes the group level of development and describes either projects, departments, organizations, communities, or cities. It is the natural "organizational form" where we work together with others in our various roles. In this book, we refer to it as the group level of co-creative processes. The All-of-us space addresses the larger society and world of which we are all a part. It is in the largest sense, our universal belonging, us as being a part of all sentient beings.

Multi-stakeholder co-creation is dependent on the creation of a shared issue

In this book, we borrow this term to describe the shared issue that is at play when a group of stakeholders meets to solve a common issue they are concerned about. This shared issue in a Collaboratory represents the stakes for the issue, the energy dynamics of a space where stakeholders work. It informs the transformative process for which the facilitator of Collaboratory processes is responsible. In his matrix of evolution, Scharmer suggests that this shared issue can enable an integration at a group level so that the group can shift from simply rule following and rule repeating to rule generating, hence the capacity of changing the game. Figure 1.4 shows these three levels of transformation with the "All of us" in the center where the Collaboratory represents

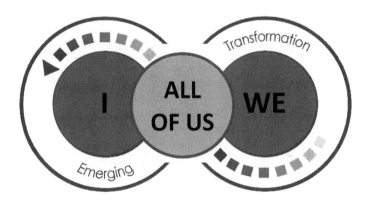

Figure 1.4 The Circle Model integrating the three levels of global responsibility

the central issue around which organizations and individuals meet. Weaving these three levels in a Collaboratory space can trigger and accelerate a transformation at all three levels.

This book clarifies the challenges of multi-stakeholder collaboration at an individual, a group, and the shared issue level; the different required steps of a collaborative process; and how to measure progress. It does not answer all questions that could be considered. When looking at the individual level, a life journey is unique and based on what families we were born into. How we were raised, what gifts and talents we developed, with what challenges we were faced, what opportunities we had? Who were our friends, for what organizations we worked, and so forth? If we were in the right place at the right time or not. As much as there is no recipe for a successful life, there is no simple recipe for how organizations can contribute to a better world.

The introspective capacity of stakeholders defines the potential of change

Much of the success of collaborative multi-stakeholder processes hinges on the introspective ability of individual participants to assess how they are contributing, what is happening in terms of group dynamics, and how things are moving to solve the common issue. It is much about moving across boundaries and accessing an interiority that allows an experience of wholeness both within oneself and with everybody around. Creating such spaces is a key concern and responsibility of the facilitator. This book offers a wider access to these challenges, enabling any individual participant to become an effective contributor. Not everybody on a multi-stakeholder team will necessarily be interested in this perspective and in spending much time on self-reflection unless proposed by the facilitator as part of the process. There is nothing like a consciousness entry exam to be taken before a person is admitted to such a process and as a result, the group will have to adapt and embrace who is present and what is possible as a result. It is part of a skillful facilitation process to bring along the development of individuals and the group so that the common issue can be addressed successfully. This may mean some decisive interventions that could, in a worst case, lead to the exclusion of a particularly destructive member.

The facilitator's role is central to creating and holding the space for stakeholder co-creation

When investigating how to overcome challenges for individuals, for groups, and the shared issue, the role of the facilitator takes central stage. While this is not a how-to-facilitate instruction book, we will point out key challenges and opportunities for facilitators along the steps and the levels of challenge.

Facilitation is the art of creating and holding spaces where transformation is possible and likely to occur. This means – centrally – that spaces of silence can be built that are pregnant of insight and reflection to trigger breakthrough new ideas and solutions. Such silences are one of the ways to measure great facilitation. There are all types of silences – lazy, tired, disengaged, distracted, exhausted, angry, defensive, and distant silences. Energetically charged, nourished, and stimulated silences take practice and time. They allow diving into what has been building silently underneath activity and conversations but has gone unnoticed due to the noise in our heads and around us. High quality moments of silences are the result of having created a safe space for participants to let go of fear and defensive mechanism so that they can fully join the unknown journey that is the path to solve wicked problems.

The role of a facilitator is to be in charge of the process, not the outcome or the content. Beyond the need to have this role clarified repeatedly, it is also important for the facilitator to be actually capable of holding up his end of that contract. For this, a facilitator of multi-stakeholder processes is aware of two separate processes:

- How is the group going in terms of individuals, group dynamics, and achieving the common goal?
- How am I doing in this?

Differentiating between these two parallel processes involves the ability to be able to empty oneself. Being an empty vessel is critical to be of service to a process. Self-observation is key as a hygiene practice of ongoing self-emptying and processing in a separate way what is building up inside that may stand in the way of facilitation. Having a journal with different columns is one way to handle this during a process. This allows a facilitator to differentiate between own reactions to what is happening in the room and what is really going on. The book does place a particular emphasis on reflective silence. Facilitators are sensitive to the energy in the room and the power of silence, and you will find insights throughout this book about how to best use it. Kathryn Goldman Schuyler has done some interesting work in understanding how such silence can contribute to transformation. It remains judgment and experience to know when to intervene and when not and how to manage the energy in the room and in which direction.

Practice and increase your self-regulation capacity as you continue

Personal integration through self-reflection is a precious aspect of this book. It is honored with specific empty pages to enable you pause and reflect and to make such integration possible. There are three pathways that address the individual level: time and space (see Chapter 3), breath (see Chapter 6) and empathy (see Chapter 9). These pathways relate in what some call "self-regulation," related to but broader then "self-efficacy," a term commonly used in positive psychology. Equally, there are three pathways to enhance efficacy. Integration at the group level for participants of group processes includes: connection (see Chapter 2), appreciation (see Chapter 4), and senses (see Chapter 7). At the shared issue level, we are looking again at three pathways. This is typically a level that facilitators focus on, but really anybody interested in developing a sensitivity in the collective consciousness can develop capacity in this domain. The related pathways are energy (Chapter 1), focus (see Chapter 5), and silence (see Chapter 8). At this level, silent resonance is the basis for the common ground needed for transformative project breakthrough. These pages offer you a space to shift from your reading mind to your sensing being. They counter-balance the writing.

You have no doubt many existing resources that you can rely on to help you in your developmental journey. The insights and inspiration that are offered in between chapters of this book hopefully enrich your personal portfolio of approaches. Some of the questions that are particularly important when looking at the developmental challenges in a multi-stakeholder process relate to gaining clarity regarding your place and your stance in a given project and process. This means reflecting on how this project relates to what you consider your place in the universe, in your life, at work, in the many roles that you hold. Stepping back to consider if the role you are holding is really a role you want to play, and can play, and if the stance you are holding is indeed helping in connecting to yourself and the issue on which you are working. Personal integration strengthens the connection to yourself, the connection to the issue, and to everything else that is.

Summary

- Society has an increasingly disruptive impact on business. Often, new realities emerge based on changing public perceptions and can overthrow the old established order in a matter of a few years. In view of a general acceleration in technology and most innovation-based trends, such disruption can be expected to both increase in speed and force. Business is well advised to broaden its risk perspective and outlook. Threats may come from unimaginable blind spots.
- Business has had an impact on society and for a long while, this impact has been considered only by a minority of activists. Increasingly, the negative impacts are scrutinized and positive impacts are gaining more visibility. Business has a choice today: to be considered the source of the problem society faces, or to be celebrated for its positive contribution to solving burning societal issues.
- The SDGs provide a framework for a global agenda and the GAPFRAME. org offers an overview of priorities by country at a glance. If change makers want to maximize their positive impact, it is of critical importance to

match their own agenda with the global agenda and the priority issues in the region in which they are active.

- Individuals have the ability to inspire the best in business. Increasingly, leadership is understood as an opportunity for anybody in any role to embrace the responsibility to contribute to the fullest of one's potential. Finding an integration of our inner values with our outer activities becomes a developmental necessity when we want to contribute to changing business and society. The circle model describes the emerging transformation that results from the interaction between the inner and outer worlds.
- Facilitating transformative processes requires an awareness and sensitive to what is going on at the individual, group, and shared issue levels. It also requires an appreciation of the power of reflection and silence as key transformative moments.
- This book offers you practical support in your personal integration journey to become the best version of yourself. There is a reflective space in between each chapter, allowing you to sense into the I, We, All-of-us spaces that define the multi-level transformational change journey this book seeks to clarify and enable.

Reflection questions

- In the country you live, what examples strike you as important when considering how society impacts business and vice versa? Share your stories and highlight lessons for business from your perspective.
- What are the biggest issues in your countries when considering environmental, societal, economic, and governance challenges? (Hint: check out www.gapframe.org and find your country).
- In the business or industry with which you are familiar, what examples are you aware of where a great leader had either a positive or negative impact on his business? Reason why.
- Where do you see your biggest potential lever for change as a person in the system: is it in your current organization, a voluntary and entrepreneurial project you are involved in, or a specific activity or project you have always wanted to implement? Tell us all about it!
- Describe a change process in which you were involved. Was the original purpose achieved? What challenges turned out to hinder progress most? What did you learn about change processes from the experience?
- How easy it is for you to connect to your needs and values and to express them transparently and non-violently when the time is right? How well do you do in ensuring other people's voices are truly heard and integrated into solutions? How conscious are you about the energy in team processes and how a group is doing as a whole over time?

Further reading and references

The Gapframe – a translator of the SDGs into national priorities for business and change makers: www.gapframe.org accessed March 30, 2018.

Goldman Schuyler, Kathryn, Skjei, Susan, Sanzgiri, Jyotsna, & Koskela, Virpi (2016): Moments of waking up: A doorway to mindfulness and presence. *Journal of Management Inquiry* 1–15.

Muff, Katrin (2017): How the circle model can purpose-orient entrepreneurial universities. *Journal of Management Development – Special Issue Entrepreneurial University* Vol 36 No 2, 146–162.

Muff, Katrin, Kapalka, Agnieszka, & Dyllick, Thomas (2017): The Gap Frame – Translating the SDGs into relevant national grand challenges for strategic business opportunities. *International Journal of Management Education* Vol 15, 363–383.

Scharmer, Otto Scharmer (2015): The Blindspot: www.huffingtonpost.com/otto-scharmer/uncovering-the-grammar-of-the-social-field_b_7524910.html

The United Nations Global Compact: www.unglobalcompact.org accessed March 30, 2018.

The United Nations: The Sustainable Development Goals (SDGs): www.un.org/sustainable development accessed March 30, 2018.

The World Business Council for Sustainable Development: www.wbcsd.org accessed March 30, 2018.

The World Economic Forum: www.weforum.org accessed March 30, 2018.

Shared issue level:

Please take a moment to reflect on your personal strengths and experiences that can serve you in this domain of change.

Energy

Please take a moment to reflect on your personal strengths and experiences that can serve you in this domain of change.

Chapter 2

The secrets of stakeholder transformation

Complex problems require appropriate practices to achieve the desired solutions

A process that vaguely resembled a Collaboratory went sour when a stakeholder group felt insulted and instrumentalized by the event organizer. The process meltdown happened when the official representative of the project initiator was kicked out of the meeting room of a neighborhood community hall. He had always felt more as a mediator or even facilitator, but the stakeholder group labeled him as instigator who allowed himself to be used in a role a respectable black man should have rejected. The black neighborhood was going to be used for the 20th anniversary of a tragic event and the white town chair thought by appointing a black representative, this would make the communication easier. Well, not at all! The black neighborhood chiefs felt that the white was just once more using them for an event for which not enough remedy had yet been done. And they were in no mood of glossing things over. The representative was unable to use his position and color as a way to bridge differences and to create a space where the participating parties could jointly see some benefits from such an event rather than sticking to only seeing competing values.

He had initially prepared what he thought was a convincing plan. It involved getting all stakeholders together and discussing a future-oriented joint project that could bring a positive spin to a tragic story. The plan worked well initially. Mostly the young generation of white and black students showed up and when they envisioned what the city could really use, they came up with some great ideas of a skateboard park and a library with no closing times. When they presented their ideas to their elders and in particularly in the black neighborhood, resistance rose. The city council was afraid that the open library would end up being used as dormitories rather than study places. The most vocal opposition, however, came from the leaders of the black neighborhood. They didn't see any benefit in these ideas which to them were at best new ways for youngsters to hang out and drink alcohol in public. They had already enough troubles at hand, they thought.

The well-intended representative had decided to also visit the home of one of the victims of the event that had occurred 20 years ago. He thought that maybe he could engage in a conversation with the elders and get them involved with some ideas for future plans. He knew that the family had great influence in the community and that things could shift if only he would get the discussion on the right topic. Things didn't go as planned. The entire tribe of the victim was present. The discussion quickly focused on the subject of insufficient financial compensation for the damages suffered. A number of distant cousins kept bringing up this issue, actively preventing any progress. Speaking of any money was the one thing the representative was not entitled to do, and they knew it. The representative felt increasingly disconnected from his task that became increasingly difficult as time went on. He couldn't go back to his superior and explain the difficulties and he could not advance.

The story illustrates what happens when particular stakeholder groups sabotage the process and how this can create a downward spiral that can lead to overall project failure. It is often the self-centered perspective that prevents finding new common ground. Wilson, who has studied sociobiology, suggests that while selfish individuals can out-compete an altruist in a group, altruistic groups have a tendency to out-compete selfish groups. While solving normal problems of a technical nature require only a basic degree of change capacity, problems that are more complex require a second-order change. Vermeesch describes second-order change as solutions that only emerge once a group has gone through a paradigmatic shift in thoughts or behavior. In fall 2017, we have witnessed a flavor of such a process breakdown. During four weeks, three parties attempted and ultimately failed to create a new German government, the so-called Jamaica coalition. The lack of ability to build trust among the parties was considered one of the underlying causes for this failure.

Solving complex problems requires groups to learn their way out in entirely new ways. The quality of the output is the result of the quality of the relationship of the space that has been created for multi-stakeholders. Bouwen adds that this includes the degree to which participants can listen, dialogue, and acknowledge each other's ideas. In the past decades of multi-stakeholder dialogues, practices such as Appreciative Inquiry, Open Space Technology, Dynamic Facilitation, and Theory U have emerged. These and others form an integral part of what we call the Collaboratory and have enabled us to shape a new understanding of how to achieve transformational change.

What unites many practices is the desire to generate conversations that disrupt the current thinking in order to generate new images so that people can see old issues from new perspectives. This is also called "changing the narrative" or the prevailing beliefs, stories, and images that shape how people in a system make meaning of new situations. Bushe and Marshak maintain that creating space for new conversations is the foundation for allowing new prototype solutions to emerge.

Stakeholders are challenged to achieve a mindset shift from competition to cooperation

To avoid cultural stereotypes, let us look at another Collaboratory process in South Africa, amended and expanded for the purpose of illustrating the shift. It was a well-prepared event that aimed at solving the conflicts in the winery industry. For months, laborers had been on strike and demanded salary improvements from the farmer. It was – once more – a black and white issue. Farmers were mostly white, laborers were mostly black. The issue was that part of salary compensation was free access to wine at the end of the day. This had a negative consequence in the surrounding black communities with increased domestic violence and a higher than normal crime rate during harvesting. The labor union demanded payment to bank accounts rather than in kind and demanded also curbing the access to wine. Many pre-meetings had already taken place, making it possible for some people to sit the same room who months earlier had accused each other in the local newspaper. The local university served as an initiator of the talks and it had organized an independent third party facilitator for the process. At the start, the atmosphere was tense among labor representatives and the representatives of the largest wineries. The neutral off-site location and a flawless process helped calm down the nerves. Using a talking stick to ensure that nobody was interrupted, predictably slowed down the conversation so that the listening could deepen.

The visioning exercise after lunch brought about a real shift. Visioning consists of letting go what we know and to connect to the larger field of all participants, imagining a future state where the problem is solved. For the first time, the two opposing parties understood the larger picture and saw the benefits of solving the issue for the local community. The most conservative wine producer openly acknowledge that he deeply cared about a safe community and that he was willing to do his part to ensure it. This statement was the beginning of both sides starting to discuss additional solutions and options including how the children could be collected from school and brought to mixed summer camps during the harvesting period, close to the wineries. Some of the women volunteered the idea of cooking community dinners that brought the otherwise isolated fathers together with the families rather than keeping them away at the farm with the risk of drinking. Finding common ground in a future vision that considered the world with the problem solved often does this trick. Conversations shift from competing values to finding ways to co-create new value together beyond what was previously thought possible. Differences that were initially considered reasons for disagreements became sources for appreciation and ideas. With the ability to step beyond defending one's own interest group to act in the interest of solving the issue, participants started to feel more connected again to their own values and what truly matters.

What is so different in this story? What has gone right here that has gone wrong in the previous story? Building on what Robert Quinn calls the normal and the fundamental leadership states, we have just witnessed here the two different states of cooperation: the state of competition and the state of collaboration. Insights from Collaboratory facilitators and practitioners suggest that there are four specific shifts that are required to create a state of collaboration in co-creation processes. These shifts from a state competition to a state of collaboration state can be described as shifting:

- From being tribe oriented to being issue oriented
- From rejecting differences to embracing differences
- From competing values to co-creating values
- From feeling disconnected to feeling connected.

The two stories describe extreme situations that seek to serve as illustrations for differentiating the two different states. Quinn suggests that a normal state is the state most of us are in most of the time. It is our standard operating mode where we are led mostly by our subconscious behavioral pattern that is often fear-based. The danger of such a normal state of behavior is obvious when a group of stakeholders meet with different priorities, perspectives, and interests. The first story has shown how little it takes for these exchanges to become self-disrupting and destructive.

Borrowing from Quinn, we are looking at two dimensions when attempting to compare what might differentiate a state of collaboration from a state of competition. Given that we are not looking at individual leadership state but states of groups, we are using the circle model as a starting aid. The inner versus outer world dimensions are useful in understanding from where the different aspects of the state originate. On one hand, we can look at how we orient our stance. Are our considerations and actions oriented internally in terms of how we see ourselves or externally triggered by how we place ourselves in relationship with others? On the other hand, there is the field of action that reflects how we express ourselves around others. Can our stance be derived from how we are in our behavior and attitude (being), or is it visible in terms of what we do through our actions and words (doing)?

When operating in a state of competition, the space is filled with inner and outer chatter

In the state of competition, stakeholders are tribe-oriented, disconnected; they reject differences and have competing values. The comfort zone for stakeholder groups means that the needs of their own organization comes first at the expense of needs and interests of others. This self-interest is placed above everything else and groups focus on what they have to gain or lose in any discussion. Their tribe comes first! In this state it is difficult to consider ideas that don't relate directly to existing market and customer reality, and there is a risk of ignoring opportunities outside of such a current vision. Stakeholders may have the opinion of holding isolated positions and they may feel marginalized or even disconnected as a result. This sense of disconnectedness is augmented in the current social media environment. Selective news and priority of opinions we agree with create a new risk of feeling disconnected. Stakeholders with minority interest risk feeling marginalized, victimized, or ignored. They risk disconnecting from the project purpose, retreating, and disengaging. Unsurprisingly, in such a state, stakeholders find it difficult to trust and work with others who hold different interests. Opinions and worldviews have been solidified over time and opinions from other groups can be rejected violently. Trust is low, particularly among those who not only have different opinions but have different interests. Competing values are difficult to overcome and can block a group of stakeholders to find a common ground to solve an issue together.

In such a state of competition, the energetic space is filled with inner and outer chatter. There is little room for silence to reflect on what is going on and there is little experience of a resonance that is happening both between me and others, and within my group of stakeholders. Figure 2.1 visualizes the state of competition.

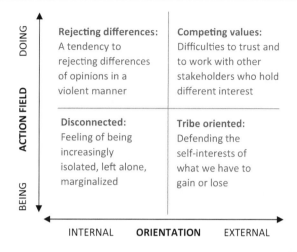

Figure 2.1 The state of competition

When operating in a state of cooperation, the space is filled with emerging resonance

When stakeholders, both individually and as a group, are able to embrace the need to change, things can change. Now, of course this is easier said than done and this book is dedicating three chapters to addressing how this might be done. When we agree to change, we agree to lose control and in a normal state of being, so argues Quinn, nobody likes to lose control. When we embrace what Quinn calls a fundamental change and are willing to embrace deep change, as a group we become issue-oriented and connected, we co-create value and embrace differences.

We will uncover what it takes for a group of stakeholders to shift from the state of competition and become connected to their higher potential and their common mission, the state of co-creation kicks in. Rather than the downward spiral of a vicious circle, the magic upward spiral of a virtuous circle emerges when superpowers kick in.

Individuals are able to transcend their personal priorities in favor of the common good and to open up for a connectivity to build with others. As groups work together, they are able to look beyond their own tribe issues and focus on the shared issue at hand with a broader view. They are able to start focusing on the common good and larger interests at stake, start looking at solutions and at what their role can be in a multi-stakeholder process. Team members are starting to express themselves with increasing authenticity.

Groups are working together to solve a shared issue experience with a sense of connectedness. They are increasingly aware of being connected to everything that is and able to collaborate with others from that stance. The previously isolated groups become open to what is happening around them. Individuals start to be able to move outside of their comfort zone and seek real feedback from others, adapting and experimenting and growing increasingly aware as part of a group process of how to work together.

Being issue-oriented implies that we are able to shift our focus to collaborating so that all of us can live well on that one planet. By looking at the issue and the related barriers and obstacles, we gain clarity that we all have to gain something from solving this issue beyond the benefits, risks, and opportunities of a single interest group. The capacity to see the benefit for all comes with a related awareness we are all somehow connected and that we are an integral part of everything that is around us. The sense of isolation diminishes and individuals are able to better participate in multi-stakeholder conversations. They start finding words to express their position and experience about the issue.

Increasingly, participants are able to hear others with new ears, and start to hear even those whose position and opinions are very different from my group or me. When a group learns to embrace such differences, the amount of violence in communication also drops. A non-violent communication practice may be a good way to ensure that everybody is able to express their own needs while being able to listen better to the needs of others. As the level of co-creation increases, the group develops an ability to work on emerging solutions with an increasing ease to embrace and deal with uncertainty. In an evolved state of co-creation, groups are at ease at co-creating value, and are able to help each other through the essential phases of uncertainty that are required to develop new values that build on existing values of different groups.

The state of co-creation is most visible in moments of stillness; this is when the emerging resonance speaks loudest. In this elevated state, individuals and groups have become accustomed and comfortable with the use of silence and it is consciously for deep conversation or reflection. As trust builds, individuals find an increasing ease to balance the contrasting needs of others and themselves in a non-violent manner, able to embrace differences. Groups demonstrate an ability to work with others on emergent solutions with ease despite continued uncertainty, able to co-create new values beyond their own. Figure 2.2 shows an overview of these four different aspects.

When comparing the two states of competition and co-creation and listening to the stories of facilitators, there are some nuggets of wisdom worth sharing. Current experience shows that successful stakeholder processes are different from unsuccessful ones in four ways: problems are solved differently, people show up differently, there is a new type of listening, and lastly, the facilitator can make or break it. Or said differently, the limitations of the facilitator determine the limits to the group process (See Table 2.1).

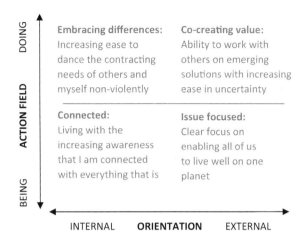

Figure 2.2 The state of co-creation

Table 2.1 Practice insights differentiating successful from unsuccessful stakeholder co-creation

State of competition	State of cooperation	Insight	Level
Tribe oriented	Issue oriented	New way of solving a problem	**Individual**
Rejecting differences	Embracing differences	Showing up differently	**Group**
Competing values	Co-creating value	New type of listening	**Common space**
Disconnected	Connected	The facilitator	

When stakeholders find new ways to work together, co-creation suddenly works

A great trick in shifting from a tribe focus to an issue orientation lies in the suggestion that the problem cannot be solved by focusing on the problem. It is often said that clearly defined problems are best solved by engineers, while more complex issues require very different, less linear approaches to new solutions. Embracing the idea of together imagining a future where the problem no longer exists, opens up new ways of looking at what this may mean to an involved group. I was involved in a stakeholder collaboration exercise in an emerging country that failed because a part of the group insisted that unless the underlying dynamics of the problem are analyzed and understood, the problem cannot be solved. All the time was spent deepening the differences of opinions, expressing differing points of view until it was no longer possible to dream of a world where the problem was resolved. While the stakeholders enjoyed having been able to express their points of view, no new breakthrough solution was achieved. In a student-led Collaboratory at a Swiss university, invited experts surprised the students with their ability to shift beyond their point of view and to quiet down into a space where a new vision could be born. In follow-on mini brainstorm sessions, these external experts showed up as true partners in imagining new solutions far beyond their own interests. A sense of common ownership and shared purpose ignited much energy for students to continue with implementing emerging ideas.

They start to show up differently and be present more authentically

Being able to show up with a different mindset is a true challenge for multi-stakeholder work. As it is not possible to select participants according to their state of personal development, it can be challenging to create a safe space where everybody feels that they can show up for who they are and what they truly represent. Such a safe space is needed as a foundation to be able to shift from rejecting to embracing differences of opinions. I have experienced a sensitive situation where a stakeholder had shared with great courage an authentic position she had experienced regarding the issue at hand, only later on to be critiqued for having used the space with a public confession. This judgmental attitude shut down the previously open and trusting space and showed to her and others the potential cost of trusting. On the other hand, I have been touched innumerous times by how people exponentially grew as a result of having connected to an inner purpose that they were able to bring into the group. I have read many reflection papers that show the miracle of what happens when there is true personal affinity with an emerging prototype and how this can change a life.

New ways of listening open the space for co-creating new value and benefits

A new type of listening is key to consider values differently and in particular to shift from competing value to co-creating value together. This is best reflected in how we listen. Do we listen with a response in mind already, or can we listen without wanting or needing to respond instantly? This is particularly challenging when sitting with a perceived enemy at the same time and trying to come to terms that we need to work together to solve the issue at hand. The Collaboratory process can help to force and to deepen real listening and can thus prepare the ground for real sharing and depth. When we broaden the horizon, we are able to step back from our own convictions and preconceptions and open up a space where we can build something new with those with whom we sit. My experience facilitating a Collaboratory session at the height of the student riots in South Africa showed how impossible this can be. Black and white students sat in a room together with university staff to discuss how to overcome the lock-down. The ongoing political situation being as it is, it was virtually impossible for a white student to share an opinion or even get a share of voice. The blacks, they insisted to be called blacks, felt that they were the only credible voice in the room with an authority to speak. They were doing upon their white fellow students what they were so enraged was being done to them. And there was no way to bring that awareness to the room at that moment in time. On the other hand, I witnessed a transformative moment in a stakeholder Collaboratory of a European mid-sized company. The group was reflecting on how change-ready they judged their organization to be and about halfway through the sharing, a junior manager who had recently joined the company spoke up. He said: "I hear so much fear in what you are saying" and went on explaining the opportunities and the upside that he saw. Calling out what was invisible yet clearly palpable in the room brought about such a relief that the entire conversation and co-creation took another spin after his courageous statement. It was his ability to listen freely and deeply, coupled with a great dose of courage, that enabled him to shift an entire process with a single sentence.

These spaces are facilitated in a way to create connection among previous strangers

The shift from a general sense of being disconnected to becoming connected is very much related to the ability to facilitate a space where such a shift is possible. Facilitation lies at the heart of this shift and experience has shown to what degree skillful facilitation is an essential ingredient of success for stakeholder processes. Experience shows that the comfort zone of the facilitator can become a limiting factor for an entire group. While the co-creation process is designed in a way to allow a very light facilitation, practice has shown that a facilitator has the power to stand in the way of a positive development of the group and to successfully advance in solving the issue.

I have witnessed a facilitator in training during a sensitive phase of a Collaboratory, the visioning process. This is a moment where participants are asked to sit comfortably and close their eyes and spend 10 minutes imagining a different future. A sensitive moment that requires a capacity to hold the space so that those not used to such a setting can relax into it. The new facilitator was insufficiently prepared for this moment and stood behind a number of participants and talked into their backs as she led the visioning exercise. The atmosphere was tense, and a number of participants shifted uncomfortably in their chairs. A few coughs and suddenly one started to giggle. That was the end. The giggling spread as a way to release tension and the visioning had to be abandoned. While unfortunate, it is of course possible to amend such a happening and this example is simply to show how important the facilitator can be in enabling or preventing the group of progress.

On the upside, I recall another Collaboratory led by students on the topic of corruption. They had managed to get representatives of all relevant NGOs into a place and the facilitator orchestrated the sharing of different perspectives in such a powerful way that the energy was nearly bubbling with readiness when the time came for the visioning. Three or four visions that were reported back from the future were put together in a subsequent brainstorming session and turned into a truly breakthrough idea that really caught fire and was implemented in the weeks after the event and still is in place.

Clearly, the role of the facilitator is important and a particular emphasis on specific suggestions will be added where possible throughout the book. The original Collaboratory book was born from the desire to develop as foolproof a process as possible to minimize the demands of a facilitator. Indeed, the knowledge and experience of a large range of such methodologies has enabled us to create a solid overall process. Having studied the facilitation of the collaborative process has enabled us to uncover the development journey that will enable these shifts at the level of the individual, the group, and the shared issue.

Effective co-creation requires an inner and outer development of first competencies and then superpowers

There is another interesting reflection, I would like to add. Watkins and Wilber discuss so-called evolutionary states and they call the process of making a heart connection, "waking up." They suggest this to be a vertical development which requires a shift from being internally closed and externally open in order to reach a heart connection with everything that is. This consciousness development occurs in any successful co-creative process at both the individual and group level at one point or the other, and the facilitator is well advised to pay particular attention to it. Goldman Schuyler has an interesting perspective on another process, that we could call "growing up." Let's imagine this as a vertical development, whereby growing up is about acquiring new skills and competencies and relates to the learning journey of any adult. These two considerations offer a map, where an individual or a group can place itself to see if they are developing more along a vertical or horizontal axis and what next development step might help them advance in their journey.

Traditional education focuses often on the horizontal development we commonly call "growing up." It is all about becoming increasingly aware of our senses, the world around us, and eventually about our place in it. Its focus is in the outer world. An often forgotten or only implicit element of education is a person's vertical development, that could also be called as "waking up." Often associated with spirituality, this personal development aspect kicks in when there are problems and challenges in life that cannot be overcome

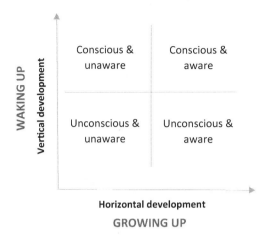

Figure 2.3 Two different development directions: waking up versus growing up

simply by an increasing amount of understanding and external contextualization. It is time to turn inward for new answers and this inner development is often also called "personal development." We have compared the importance of a development of the inner and the outer world in Chapter 1. Figure 2.3 offers a visualization of these two developmental movements.

Quinn has described four different ways of considering leadership development. He suggests that there is a static view, a polar view, a competing values view, and an integrated view. These dimensions are equally relevant for group development.

The static view suggests that a successful Collaboratory can be described in a list of desirable traits and attributes. A participant is influential, appreciative, and engaged. An effective group of stakeholders can envision an ideal solution, embrace complexity, and achieve an Efficacy. The shared issue of a multi-stakeholder project is an adaptive space, consisting of high coherence, disruptive ideas, and enabling a heart connection.

The polar view takes these attributes and traits from the static view and arranges them in polar groups, seemingly opposite in nature, but also with some kind of underlying connection. This view offers a more complex and dynamic way of deciphering ideal traits and attributes. For example, a participant is both investigative and caring; a stakeholder group is able to have a high coherence and handle disruptive ideas; a shared issue is both structured and adaptive.

The competing values view seeks to align polarities that are similar to each other and explains how each of them can turn into a limiting factor when overemphasized. It introduces the idea that each positive trait or attribute can also have a negative side. It represents a more dynamic view than the first two views as it also requires a reflection about positive and negative expressions of attributes.

The integrated view takes the traits and attributes that have been established, grouped, and analyzed in the first three views. It suggests that integrating the positive sides of two competing polar traits results in the creation of a superpower. Here we suggest calling these strength polarities that can be integrated to shift from a state of competition to a state of collaboration.

The next three chapters are dedicated to exploring what these strengths polarities look like at the individual, the group, and the shared issue levels.

Summary

- When stakeholders meet and work together on a tricky issue, they typically work together in a state of competition. This is really the normal stance that people working together bring to the table. People and groups are tribe oriented, rejecting differences of others, bring competing values, and often have a sense of feeling disconnected personally or as a group from the larger project and purpose.
- An effective and successful multi-stakeholder space is defined by a shift in these four elements. People and groups shift from being tribe oriented to being issue oriented, rather than rejecting differences they start embracing them, they move beyond competing values to being able to co-create value, and as a result start to feel connected more deeply within themselves, to the others in the project, and to the overall cause.
- Insights from Collaboratory experiences suggest some priorities in how to achieve these required shifts. At the individual level, there is a need to become open to a new way of solving a problem beyond only seeing all the issues, which helps shifting from a tribe to an issue orientation. At the group level, the ability to show up differently, to be reflective about oneself and the role of others allows a shift from rejecting to embracing differences of opinions. And at a shared issue level, a deeper listening allows stakeholders to move from focusing on competing values to opening up to co-creating value together.
- Looking at the three dimensions of the personal, the organizational, and the societal, or the I, We, and All-of-us is a useful way to consider how these shifts from a state of competition to a state of cooperation can be achieved. In addition, the facilitator who is in charge of generating a process that enables progress and transformation in each of the three levels, also is holding the space for the group and individuals to connect to each other, themselves, and the issue. This underlying condition for change results in trust being generated, so that people can show up with courage and vulnerability.

- Lessons learned from many stories have allowed us to identify key traits and attributes at the three levels. They also enabled us to group them as polar opposites. The two opposites represent the full spectrum of the related strength polarities. When integrated into a superpower, these strength polarities provide pathways toward a successful multi-stakeholder co-creative process. The next three chapters are dedicated to these pathways by looking at the level of the individual, the group, and the shared issue.

Reflection questions

- Can you relate to the state of competition when reflecting on how it is to work with others, particularly other stakeholders with different perspectives and priorities? And if so, what elements resonate with you and what other issues occur to you?
- Do you remember having been in a state of collaboration when working with others? Do you recall the atmosphere and feeling in the room, how much lighter and easier everything was? What else do you remember and what was different in you during these moments?
- What do you take away from this chapter in how you can show up differently to a next stakeholder meeting? To what will you pay more attention?
- Where would you place yourself in the vertical versus horizontal development map? And what might help you advance as a next step?
- Do you have any facilitation experience, and would you be interested in acquiring more experience? If so, do you see an opportunity to gather some people around an issue about which you care, no matter how small it is, and test how you can create a space of collaboration? The next chapters will help you in what to pay attention to.

Further reading and references

Bouwen, R., & Taillieu, T. (2004): Multi-party collaboration as social learning for interdependence: Developing relational knowing for sustainable natural resource management. *Journal of Community & Applied Social Psychology* Vol 14 No 3, 137–153.

Bushe, Gervase R., & Marshak, Robert J. (2015): The dialogic mindset in organization development. The dialogic mindset in organization development. *Research in Organizational Change and Development* Vol 22, 55–97.

Goldman Schuyler, Kathryn, Skjei, Susan, Sanzgiri, Jyotsna, & Koskela, Virpi (2016): Moments of waking up: A doorway to mindfulness and presence. *Journal of Management Inquiry*, 1–15.

Quinn, Robert E. (2004): *Building the bridge as you walk on it*. Jossey Bass, San Francisco.

Vermeesch, Inge, Art, Dewulf, Marc, Craps, & Katrien, Termeer (2013): A relational perspective on leadership in multi-actor governance networks for sustainable materials management. *Towards a Framework Based on Complexity Leadership Paper Presented at the 1st*

International Conference on Public Policy Grenoble June 26–28, 2013. http://archives.ippa publicpolicy.org/IMG/pdf/panel_43_s1_vermeesch.pdf last accessed July 29, 2018.

Watkins, Alan, & Wilber, Ken (2015): *Wicked and wise – how to solve the world's toughest problems*. Urban Publishing, Croydon.

Wilson, David S. (2007): Rethinking the theoretical foundation of sociobiology. *The Quarterly Review of Biology* Vol 82 No 4, 327–348.

Group level:

Please take a moment to reflect on your personal strengths and experiences that can serve you in this domain of change.

Connection

Please take a moment to reflect on your personal strengths and experiences that can serve you in this domain of change.

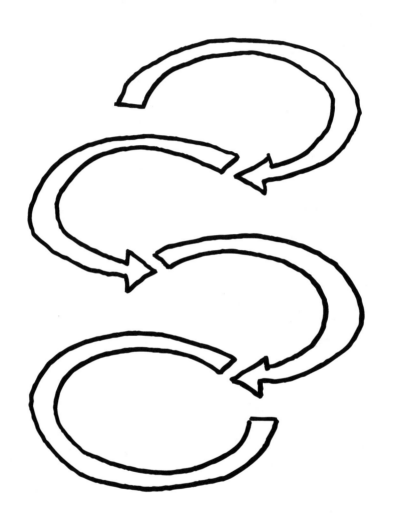

Part II

Challenges and solutions for stakeholder co-creation

Our research and experience shows that when strengths are overstretched, they can turn into limitations. These are often a cause for conflict and process breakdown. When we can return from these limitations to their underlying strengths, broken or fragile co-creation processes can be stabilized. Superpowers emerge when strengths are matched and reinforced. Sometimes this happens naturally and we all know people with such superpowers. Other times, these need to be developed and trained. This part provides easy steps in each relevant dimensions of stakeholder co-creation and highlights three superpowers in these dimensions.

Chapter 3 *suggests three pathways for advancing an individual contribution in a stakeholder gathering to provide a genuine engagement to the project and others. Stories illustrate the challenges that emerge when we want to bring in the strength and we take a good look at what happens when strengths are overemphasized and becoming a limiting factor for the process. Becoming aware of one's tendencies between strength polarities and the risk an unbalanced emphasis has, allows stepping forward in attempting to integrate competing polarities into their superpowers.*

Chapter 4 *follows the same logic as* Chapter 3 *and identifies pathways at the group level. Here group dynamics come into play and the attention is focused on what happens among stakeholder groups rather than for an individual alone. Here also, an overemphasized strength becomes a limit and the chapter allows you to assess your ability to positively express strength. Integrating a strength polarity into a superpower provides clarity on how a group can engage in collective solutions.*

Chapter 5 *considers the pathways toward transformative spaces from an issue's perspective. What is needed so that individuals and groups can work together across the various stages of co-creation? How can harmony and disruption balance each other and how can a facilitator provide both a structured and a flexible space? The competing strength polarities are explored in stories of co-creation moments. Concrete suggestions for the facilitator seek to avoid limitations and find the superpowers of competing polarities when and where needed.*

Figure II.1 *shows an overview of the insights and learnings of the three chapters of this part of the book: the superpowers for individuals, groups, and for the entire process itself. These superpowers are the results of two opposing strengths integrating into a higher level of coherence – hence, superpowers. What is interesting is what lies behind these strengths. We started noticing that conflicts in co-creation processes were often triggered by people overexpressing a natural strength they possessed, which by itself was perfect but in collaboration with others triggered negative reactions and most often other people ended up overstretching other strengths to counter-balance. We realized that the best way out of conflicts is to remind people of the underlying original strength and to then enrich that particular strength with its polar opposite in order to create awareness of the breadth of expression of potential. When pairing such opposite strengths and when learning to navigate between the best versions of both, something magic happens. A new, higher level coherence appears. Let's call them superpowers.*

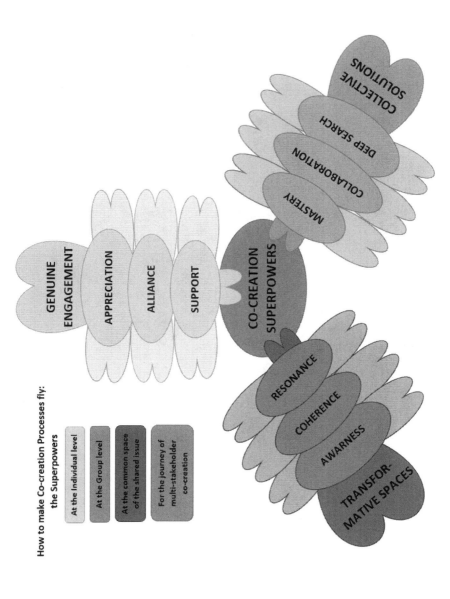

How to make Co-creation Processes fly: the Superpowers

At the Individual level

At the Group level

At the common space of the shared issue

For the journey of multi-stakeholder co-creation

GENUINE ENGAGEMENT

APPRECIATION

ALLIANCE

SUPPORT

CO-CREATION SUPERPOWERS

MASTERY

COLLABORATION

DEEP SEARCH

COLLECTIVE SOLUTIONS

RESONANCE

COHERENCE

AWARNESS

TRANSFOR-MATIVE SPACES

Figure II.1 The superpowers of multi-stakeholder co-creation processes

Chapter 3

Superpower #1 – genuine engagement of individuals

Overcoming the need to be right and to judge others is a challenge for individuals

In a Swiss Collaboratory where industry experts met to jointly assess opportunity for a coalition in the area of food waste, an interesting clash of characters occurred. The initiator had invited an expert on the topic who stepped into the process believing that he held all the answers and was asked to contribute the proven solutions he knew. During an early explorative discussion in smaller groups, an activist challenged him to prefer a certain way of solving the problem while ignoring some serious negative consequences. The expert was baffled and taken aback. He strongly felt that as a proven authority in his field, he knows about the ins and out of the topic and he cannot be questioned by a youngster who obviously had no clue. The activist got support from two students who felt he had a point. The expert became red in his face and stood up. He was looking for the initiator. He walked out of the discussion and complained to the initiator how ungrateful the participants were and how ignorant of solutions he presented. While the initiator felt that the expert was mostly concerned about how being challenged reflected on the expert's creditability and his possible fear of damaging his reputation, he didn't quite know how to handle the situation. The students had a point, he felt, and it was exactly the diversity of opinions that enriched the process. This was what he had hoped for and he was a bit irritated by expert not being able to be more open. He told the expert exactly this and repeated that he had invited him to bring in his expertise and not to impose his opinion. The expert was hurt. He felt misunderstood and rejected with his valid request for help. The initiator cared very deeply about food waste and it had taken him four months to gain the trust from all the industry experts and the activists to join. He felt that things were not going the right way and regretted not having a facilitator present who could bring a neutral energy to the dispute. The initiator clapped into his hands and reminded everybody that the point of the discussion was for everybody to listen openly to the opinion of others, to not interrupt each other by using the "speaking stone," and to give space so that everybody's opinion could be heard. The activist and the students made a noise that meant "who are you kidding!" and stepped out for a break. When they got up, others took this as a moment to loosen their legs and grab a cup of coffee and slowly but surely the exercise drizzled out. The initiator was at a loss of how to continue. He knew he needed to ensure the expert stayed, but he also wanted the students to stay. But how?

When listening to the challenges of individual participants of collaborative change processes, we notice that a strength of an individual can easily turn into a limiting factor in such a process. Table 3.1 summarizes these individual limitations from the preceding story.

When looking at the preceding story, we can see how the strengths of two participants turned into limitations for both of them and for the process overall:

- **A:** The "expert" has a strength to be critical; this can turn into a limitation when he feels self-righteous and fears he might be challenged in his authority.
- **B:** The project "optimist" brings the strength of being integrated and positive, which can turn into a limitation when he becomes frustrated about others putting their own opinions before the project.

What is interesting to note is that the limiting expressions of both strengths bear some similarities in themselves: being closed as a result of feeling self-righteous is not that different from being judgmental as a result of feeling frustrated (see Figure 3.1). We all have experience in how irritating people

Table 3.1 First example of opposing limitations at the individual level

1st example of opposing limitations at the individual level	
1	A: I know and I am right and my authority and expertise cannot be questioned – I can only lose out here	B: I really believe in this project – why can't everybody be open and listen to another – the project will fail if everybody sticks to their opinions

Figure 3.1 The polarity switch of two opposing limitations into a strength polarity

can be who are the seeming opposite to how we perceive ourselves or to what our values are. Seeing the resembling sameness in the other is a key for finding oneself back to one's strength rather than seeing the world from one's limitation. Rather than judging the other for being self-righteous and closed, the challenge is about finding the path back to one's integrity. And rather than closing up and distancing oneself for feeling judged by others, the path to a positive contribution lies in finding the path back to one's realistic mindset.

Let us consider a second story.

In a Collaboratory in a medium-sized city in Europe the city council had invited a number of large, medium, and small organizations to get together around how to bring a Common Good movement as part of upcoming city celebrations. The various participants had already met a few times and remained stuck on some of the ideas. The initiator felt that some participants were not quite honest in disclosing their personal feelings about some alternatives discussed and were sabotaging the project. He said so during a check-in. One of the executives who felt accused instantly used her talking slot to defend herself. She said: "I am glad to have my organization contribute to this project, however, I am certainly not here to explore everybody's motives and emotions about what is on the table. This is a collaboration project not group therapy!" She rejected the idea that there might be value in looking at why she and a few others had been spending the entire morning blocking an idea that others felt was simply brilliant. It was obvious that she was worried about an aspect that could be re-arranged or avoided, if only she would dare to admit what her real issue was. She didn't want to expose herself and was ready to leave the group if things were not managed more "professionally." She stopped allowing her curiosity to drive new ideas and became increasingly irritated and impatient. It came to a point where a mechanical compromise would be the only way forward. A participant who had previously taken the risk of exposing herself by sharing a personal story felt rejected. She had contributed to the project options by sharing how important an element of the project was to her.

She had told the story of how this had enabled her to reconnect her son to his job and for her to feel integrated as a mother, even if her company was not particularly pleased. Hearing that emotions were not welcome meant to her that it was stupid to have shared her story. She felt cheated by the process which she had assumed would be safe. How could she work with others if what she said was not protected? She felt exposed and vulnerable in a way that made her want to leave. The initiator saw this reaction and looked for the facilitator for how to continue.

Collaboratory participants have shared these and similar stories with us over the years when we looked at identifying challenges that prevent a successful multi-stakeholder process. Table 3.2 summarizes these limitations emerging from the second story.

What is important is to understand that each of these has an underlying strength at their source.

- **C:** The "professional" has a particular strength to drive processes along in a great way. However, this drive can become limiting to the group's process when she is unwilling to be more open and engage in other dimensions than the all-important facts and figures, refusing to reflect on her own feelings and concerns. Her impatience may severely limit true new insights that come from unexpected moments of sharing.
- **D:** The "care giver" brings as a strength the ability to be caring and engaged, which in turn can be limiting for the group when for the sake of bringing harmony to the group, he may sacrifice his own truth and authentic perspective, becoming overbearing to others.

Each strength can end up being a weakness when not framed in the context of an opposing strength. Or expressed differently: each limiting behavior represents a hidden strength that awaits being called forth. We call this phenomenon a strength polarity, as is outlined in Figure 3.2.

For individual participants, there are a number of such opposing polarities and their related strength polarities. A further important polarity that has emerged from our experience is highlighted in Figure 3.3. It highlights

Table 3.2 Second example of opposing limitations at the individual level

2nd example of opposing limitations at the individual level	
2 C: I don't see the benefits of bringing in feelings and to engage beyond my professional role – I want to advance solving the problem and not engage in group therapy!	D: I am willing to share my own feelings and concerns about this issue but I am worried about how vulnerable this makes me. I expect others to expose themselves too.

Figure 3.2 The polarity switch of two opposing limitations into a strength polarity

Figure 3.3 The polarity switch of two opposing limitations into a strength polarity

the dynamics of what happens when participants fall back into their limitations and become either opinionated or unprincipled. The developmental journey for them is to find the path back to their related strength and express themselves as the powerful influencer and inclusive bridge builders they can also be.

Genuine engagement develops when participants turn their strengths into superpowers

These strength polarities were developed by triangulating the insights from interviews of Collaboratory practitioners, insights from the relevant personal development literature and my own experience. As we dive into the subtleties of these polarities, I will also share insights from the literature in each of these strength polarities. As a result, it was possible to identify the different elements that contribute to enable an individual participant to express genuine engagement. These elements are reflected in strength polarities. Each of these represent a set of keys for Collaboratory participants to self-assess their own progress in being an effective partner. We will now look at each of the underlying three strength polarities (see Figure 3.4).

In the spirit of a strength-based approach, we shall focus on the challenges that have to do with overcoming the competing strength polarities and the journey of integrating two strengths into a superpower. This is not to say that the awareness does not also include having to find the path back to these two strengths if a situation pushes us into a limiting expression of these, as outlined earlier. The bigger challenge, however, is to work on the strength polarities so that an individual participant can be of **Genuine Engagement** to a multi-stakeholder co-creation project. Genuine engagement means a variety of things that we will dissect into complementary underlying dimensions of polarities. Robert Quinn calls the integration of such competing strength a

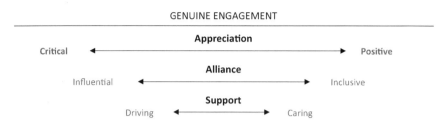

Figure 3.4 The strength polarities and superpowers at the individual level

"creative state," and here such a positive integration of the strength polarity results in a superpower that we call "Genuine Engagement."

Appreciation results from being critical and positive, overcoming self-righteous judgment

Appreciation is about the ability to integrate the value of being Critical, with the value of being Positive and encouraging. There is clear value in both of these strength polarities. There is a developmental journey behind both of these. The challenge of moving a critical perspective toward finding a positive and constructive approach lies in the ability to translate the message in such a way that it can be received. It is about moving beyond "knowing it better" to suggesting that there may be a third perspective to be explored beyond the original argument and the critic. This requires a genuine openness to discover a new perspective, essential for a genuine engagement. On the other side of the coin, shifting being positive to being genuinely engaged requires the translation of open-mindedness, and hence the risk of just going with the wind in favor of advancing, into a genuine engagement which includes taking a stance where important. Many of us will possess a bit of both these strengths. Depending on the situation and the issue at stake, we may be more on the critical side, or more on the positive side. Strength polarities are invitations to self-observe where we are at any given point in a process and in particular when our point of view is challenged (see Figure 3.5).

When looking at the strength polarity of **Critical** versus **Positive**, Robert Quinn defines the ability to conduct a critical inquiry and research as a positive leadership trait. He describes the developmental journey from a potentially destructive or pessimistic expression of inquiry to a critical and realistic approach. This illustrates the stretch between what a practitioner describes as a limiting behavior of another member and the potential expression of the related strength. The critical mind of inquiry is invaluable. The journey of becoming Critical involves shifting from the disruptive aspect of being self-righteous when feeling at odds with a situation to finding a Critical stance. On the other hand, Robert Quinn talks about

Figure 3.5 From strength polarity to Superpower

self-actualization when describing the developmental journey of becoming appreciative and open. This involves a shift away from the destructive effect of being judgmental.

Alliance happens when an inclusive influencer stops being opinionated or unprincipled

In the second polarity pair, one strength describes a person who is particularly **influential** and where the challenge lies in finding a way to use one's voice to serve as a positive reference for a shared dream. On the other side is the strength of somebody who is **inclusive**, with a talent of building quality connections, so that clusters of isolated groups can be dissolved. Both of these are undoubtedly invaluable strengths. An influential person may be somebody who is great at expressing an important opinion, even at the risk of being isolated, yet knowing how to play the power game in such a way that there may be isolated persons left behind. An inclusive person, on the other hand, may sacrifice expressing his opinion at the expense of wanting to build bridges. While he knows the power of compromise and dialogue, he needs to be careful not to be perceived as unprincipled in his effort of bringing people together. The challenge here lies in overcoming the limiting effects of these strengths. How can you use your voice to serve as a positive reference while building connections? Depending on the situation, you will find yourself more focused on one or the other of these two. Keeping an eye on where you are at and observing yourself will help you become more masterful (see Figure 3.6).

Insights from the literature illuminate the competing strengths of being influential and of being inclusive. Watkins and Wilber describe being reputable as being able to find your voice with the challenge of shifting from being ignored or not being heard to being referenced and finding some centrality in the discussion through your voice. On the other hand, they describe bridging as the journey from being a disruption to the process to becoming a true contribution. From being disconnected and isolated to being able to be inclusive and so to bridge clusters and increase the quality of the connections. We have used their insights to develop our strength polarities, enriching their insights with stories of participants.

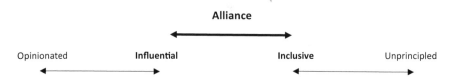

Figure 3.6 From strength polarity to Superpower

Support comes from being open and caring, resisting the temptation to be distant and impatient

The third strength polarity toward Support is to be open and caring. The strength of being **Open** involves the challenge of shifting an investigative mind into a curious and open mind. Being open requires to avoid being perceived as withdrawn as a result of possibly having over-engaged and to overcome this reaction in an authentic way. **Caring**, on the other hand, involves the journey from being distant when things are not going as we feel is right to finding ways of being empathic toward others in an authentic and centered way. Both of these strengths are extraordinary and possibly closer connected than the previous strength polarities, as both of them require an advanced degree of self-reflection. As we can see, both strengths carry in themselves their own challenge. It is worth asking yourself where you would place yourself on the spectrum and how much integration work you have at which extreme of these two. If you find yourself on the side of being very much caring about the process, this preference may come at the expense of not entirely expressing all the doubts that you may have and hence becoming distant. On the other hand, you may be wondering to what degree you are really able to be open about other people having other opinions. You can ask yourself: "In what situation am I more open and live with differences in an authentic way, and when am I more on the caring side, being at peace with myself, and being able to critically and positively approach others?" Consider Figure 3.7.

I have listened to stories of ruthless or inconsiderate behavior that has caused disruption in a Collaboratory process and yet, what we are looking for is not the absence of such people but the transformation of the limiting expression into its strength so that they can shift toward a positive and integrated approach. Howard Gardner has looked at different types of intelligence and defines emotional intelligence as an important counterpart to intellectual intelligence. He outlines the developmental journey from a potentially disruptive to an open and caring expression as overcoming being distant and withdrawn to others in a journey toward integration.

Appreciation, Alliance, and Support are superpowers for Genuine Engagement

In many ways, these strength polarities offer pathways to integrate the over-arching strength polarity for individuals to become partners by providing Genuine Engagement.

What does this tell us about how to ensure to be a positive force and to contribute genuine engagement to a collaborative multi-stakeholder project? We can summarize Figure 3.8 by identifying the superpower of the four competing strength pairs that serve as pathways to achieve a spirit of genuine engagement. The superpower of the strength pair Critical versus Positive is called **Appreciation**. Such a stance is the result of being both critical about what is going on and what is developed while being able to find the strength and patience to express a critical opinion in a critical, positive way. The strength polarity of being influential versus inclusive can be integrated into a superpower called **Alliance**. A bridge builder creates alliances and has influence in the group and hence being listened to, while also being conscious of how to include isolated views or groups in such a way that bridges can be built on the path toward collective solutions. Integrating the strength duo being open and caring leads to **Support**. This is a playful and open way of being present with a group, able to ask challenging questions while at the same time remaining fully engaged in a caring and authentic way. Figure 3.9 is a visual way of showing the superpowers.

Figure 3.7 From strength polarity to Superpower

Individual level:

GENUINE ENGAGEMENT

Strength polarity		Super power
Constructive	Positive	**Appreciation**
Influential	Inclusive	**Alliance**
Driving	Caring	**Support**

Figure 3.8 Overview of individual level strength polarities and superpowers

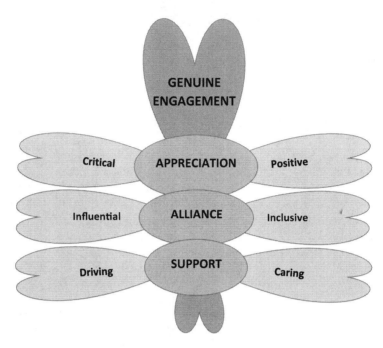

Figure 3.9 Visual overview of individual level strength polarities and superpowers

Summary

- Insights from Collaboratory facilitators or participants, from the literature and from my own experience as a Collaboratory practitioner allow defining different pathway to become an effective partner in collaborative process. These pathways have to do with translating limiting behaviors into their original strengths and with integrating competing strength polarities into a superpower.
- The superpower of individuals is to live genuine engagement. This can be achieved through the three superpowers Appreciation, Alliance, and Support. Each of these superpowers are the result of having combined two opposing strengths into a higher state. Each of these are pathways for providing genuine engagement to your next collaborative team project.
- Being Critical is connected with other strengths such as being influential and being open.
- Being Positive is related to being inclusive and caring.
- Each strength polarity can ideally be integrated into a superpower, and requires having looked at the blind spots of the limiting expressions of underlying strengths.

Reflection questions

- Refer to Figure 3.4 and imagine on which of the two sides you more likely have your strength on a good day when working in a group of multiple stakeholders. Ask yourself the following two questions to know where to place the **circle** on each of the four lines:

  - First ask yourself: which strength is more dominant in me (left or right side)?
  - Then ask yourself: do I live the circled strength more as a positive or a limiting expression (which side of the vertical line within a strength polarity: toward the center for a positive expression, toward the outside for a limiting expression)?

Repeat this for the other levels.

- Using the same Figures 3.5, 3.6, and 3.7, imagine what happens when adversity strikes and you get pushed into a corner. Most likely you will find yourself on the outer right or left sides of the vertical line. Place a **cross** at the point of the limitations you see yourself expressing more naturally. You could find yourself either on the same strength as above on the opposite side.

Repeat this for the other levels.

- Look at what picture presents itself across all the four levels. What emerges for you and what learnings and insights can you generate for yourself? While you may have an advanced degree of integration in one or the other level, you may remind yourself to pay more attention to how you balance yourself between two strengths and how you can find your own center again when you get carried away in a challenging situation.
- You now have an overview of your key personal challenges to integrate polarities on your journey toward providing genuine engagement as a participant to a project. Now it is a question of practice and self-reflection to further develop your competencies.
- If you are currently participating in a co-creative multi-stakeholder process, here are some useful questions to ask yourself about each of the four levels:

  - How have I concretely managed to move toward a further integration here?
  - Where do I want to pay more attention in my own attitude and action?
  - What best practice examples have I observed among other participants in this tension pair?
  - How will I noticeably honor a moment where another member lived a moment of perfect integration?

Further reading and references

Gardner, Howard (1997): *Extraordinary minds – portraits of four exceptional individuals and an examination of our own extraordinariness.* Basic book, New York.

Goleman, Daniel (1998): *Working with emotional intelligence.* Bantam, New York.

Quinn, Robert E. (2004): *Building the bridge as you walk on it.* Jossey Bass, San Francisco.

Watkins, Alan, & Wilber, Ken (2015): *Wicked and wise – how to solve the world's toughest problems.* Urban Publishing, Croydon.

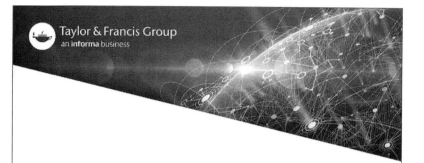

Individual level:

Please take a moment to reflect on your personal strengths and experiences that can serve you in this domain of change.

Time – space

Please take a moment to reflect on your personal strengths and experiences that can serve you in this domain of change.

Chapter 4

Superpower #2 – collective solutions of groups

Finding the right balance between analyzing the problem versus visioning is a group challenge

In a developing country, there was a collaborative session of a special kind. Experts from abroad were invited to participate both from a process perspective and to help untangle a complex local issue that stakeholders recognized was stuck. Some of the international experts believed that their best contribution was to shed light on the underlying symptoms of the problem in a very theoretical and abstract manner. This belief interfered with the process which envisioned that the local stakeholders would spend time imagining together what a better future would look like. When the international experts insisted that the only way to advance was to first dig into the problem and not to jump into the future, a number of local stakeholders became impatient. They felt that the international experts were distracting the process and what they proposed to be a waste of time. History had shown that trying to understand the problem wouldn't lead anywhere. Finally having so many different parties in one room was such an opportunity to try something new and promising. They wanted future-visioning process to go on and not hear from the international experts and their theoretical assumptions of the problems in their country. The international experts got quite upset and felt questioned in their authority. They called for a break, gathered together in a corner and debated. The facilitator who had planned the future-oriented activity was not included. When they returned they announced that they would leave the process if their point would not be taken into account and more time was not spent on understanding the underlying issues. In their view, it was impossible to have different participating groups simply share their perspectives and points of view in an attempt to then develop a shared common vision.

Their strong belief was that in order to solve a problem, the underlying symptoms must be analyzed and understood. The issue was not whether they were right or wrong, the issue was that their insistence of being right threatened to break down the process. The other people in the room equally insisted and wanted to advance with expressing the various perspectives and points of view on the room. They also insisted on being right. The initiator of the project was absent which created a leadership vacuum. It was he who had called in the international experts and some local stakeholders felt obliged to respect their guests. When he came back, not understanding what really had happened, he invited the international guests to take over facilitation and continue how they argued was best. The process disintegrated over the afternoon and there was no follow-up possible among the local stakeholders. The activities of the next day were canceled and a decision on how to continue put into the future.

As this story illustrates, there are challenges in the group process that need attention if we want multi-stakeholder projects to succeed. This chapter looks at these and provides pathways for addressing and overcoming them. At the group level, our focus expands from the individual contribution to include also challenges that relate to the role a person or a number of persons assume as they represent specific organizations in the process. A challenge of group dynamics relates also to the fact that the members of such processes are not stable, some people may be a part of the process early on, others may join mid-way, some may leave along the way.

Table 4.1 illustrates the challenges and limitations of such group dynamics and how they can be detrimental when opposing perspective clash.

Let us look at how these limitations are actually founded in important strengths that are of great service to the co-creation process. When a strength

Table 4.1 First example of opposing limitations at the group level

1st example of opposing limitations at the group level	
1 A: The issue is much more complex than is understood by the individuals and groups presented here. If we don't understand the underlying societal dynamics, there is no point in attempting to solve this issue.	B: There is a powerful process that builds on a shared ideal future vision that includes everybody's dreams – we must stick to this process and move beyond trying to dig into the details of the problem again and again.

becomes too pronounced, it can turn into an expression that can limit a group. Let us look here how that might have happened in the preceding story:

- **A:** The "historian" brings a strength of analyzing and understanding the underlying symptoms of complex issues, and this strength can turn into a limitation when he insists that understanding and resolving these symptoms is the only way to advance and proceed.
- **B:** The "visionary" has a strength that lies in overcoming differences by focusing on what a shared dream of an ideal solution might look like that he knows will bring new solutions to an old problem. This strength can turn into a limitation when he expresses rigidity about wanting to advance strictly with the envisioned process with the risk of leaving others behind which may then jeopardize the continuation of the project.

The connection of these strengths and the risk of a limiting expression are shown below in Figure 4.1. As we have seen previously, the tension here is an entirely different process of understanding. One perspective insists that only by understanding the problem will we advance, while the other perspective insists that only be letting go of the problem and focusing on ideal solutions will the breakthrough occur. Both positions are equally challenging as ultimately they insist there is only one right way and unless everybody agrees, there is no way forward. The challenges with this polarity pair is to find the path back from insisting to be right about how to go about solving an issue to returning to both underlying strengths. Those with an ability to understand underlying symptoms can build on that strength to see the value of another point of view as one avenue of advancing. Those with the strength of envisioning a solution will recognize that it is important to have everybody on board when taking that journey and that there is value in listening to other divergent thoughts. The path for both is really to find a way to embrace collective solutions in solving the issue at hand, and this search has many dimensions that need to be embraced. On one hand, the development journey for a group will consist of letting go of solely focusing on the problem, while contributing with the analytical skills to ensure the situation is fully understood. On the other hand, there may be members of a group that are stuck in dreaming up impossible and detached visions and who will be challenged to ensure that envisioning new solutions is anchored in the context of the situation. We will see further along how combining the two strengths is true magic to the process.

Figure 4.1 The polarity switch of two opposing limitations into a strength polarity

Let us better understand how challenges at the group level are different from challenges at the individual level (see previous chapter). To illustrate the challenges of an individual group member, here are questions that fellow facilitators have shared with me:

- **On an individual level:** What is at stake and what are my various roles in this process? Am I closing discussions or am I opening discussions? Am I focusing on differences between others and my group's perspective, or am I able to listen openly to what other groups have to say?
- **At a group level:** What is at stake for me as a member of a group if we succeed or we fail with this process? How does this reflect on our group and how does this reflect on me as a member of this group? To whom do I report and what are external pressures on me or on the group that may be obvious to me but not to others in my group? To what degree can I make such external expectations transparent, and how can this be helpful in clarifying open or hidden tensions in the process?
- **Regarding the process:** How does this process and the emerging solutions challenge the perspective, the motives, and motivations of the group to which I belong? How do these possibly challenge my continuous participation in the process? How can I share my concerns without endangering the continuation of this process?

These questions are what is at stake at the group level of the developmental journey of a co-creative stakeholder process. The following concrete example further illustrates the limiting outcomes of such challenges. We shall then anchor both of these limitations in their underlying strengths and the potential of their strength polarities.

In this particular setting, there was an important stakeholder that was represented by two individuals who were new to co-creation processes. After the morning session which involved processes they had never before experienced, the two felt destabilized and had discussed their discomfort during lunch. They felt they were losing control and were nervous about what to report back to their boss when returning to work after the end of this co-creative day. Not surprisingly, they showed up in the afternoon with a different energy. In the check-in round, one of them said: "How can I be expected to represent my organization in a process I have little say in and where the outcome is unknown? It may not be in the best interest of my company to be present here! I need some assurances that I can control the process outcome, I cannot expose my organization to such a risky process and I don't know if it is responsible

for me to continue here." Naming his fear gave space to others to feel their fear, too. Another participant from an opposing stakeholder group who had been nervously watching the two all morning, jumped in. He was quite emotional and said that unless the participants' groups are open to new solutions that go beyond defending a single interest, there is no point in this entire adventure. He made a big point about how complex issues require new types of solutions and that there is no way upfront to ensure that every single group can be satisfied. He appealed to a sense of personal ownership and of courage that everybody had to bring in. His voice rose and some of the participants leaned back and crossed their arms, expressing discomfort. He was adamant about everybody needing to see beyond divergent interests to find a solution and that prototyping was the only way forward to such new solutions. The facilitator was required to interrupt the planned next exercise and find a way for everybody to be reassured about the process and its purpose.

This story shows how two different stakeholders expressed opposing concerns in a way that threatened the group process. Imagine if on top of this complex situation, there might have been a disagreement among the representatives of a stakeholder. The challenges of such group dynamics can amplify issues at the individual level, adding a level of complexity. Table 4.2 illustrates the two opposing positions in the above example:

These limitations reflect real situations we have experienced in Collaboratory situations. The trick here is to focus on each of the underlying strengths that is hidden underneath these opposing limitations.

- **C:** The "controller" has a strength of understanding that issues are complex and wicked and that an outcome cannot be predicted or anticipated. This knowledge can become limiting when it is combined with the fear

Table 4.2 Two examples of opposing limitations at the group level

2nd example of opposing limitations at the group level	
2 C: How can I be expected to represent my organization in a process that I have no control over and where the outcome is unknown and may not be in our best interest – I don't control the outcome and I can't expose my organization to such a risk.	D: The issue can only be resolved if participating groups are open to new solutions that don't yet exist – these will not satisfy every single interest – we must see beyond diverging interests to fix the issue.

that the singular interest that he represents may be at risk and that he may not have full control of the outcome.

- **D:** The "prototyper" is particularly strong in embracing uncertainty and knowing that it is only through open exploration and by letting go of preconceptions that truly new solutions can emerge. This strength can turn into a limitation when he finds that people or sub-groups resist this open collaborative process and he will be harsh in judgment when he senses that interest groups defend their own interests as a priority.

These two opposing strengths can obviously fire off some quite challenging group dynamics, as we have seen in the previous example. The two different and relevant perspectives suggest that solving a problem may be so complex that one can get overwhelmed and will slide into a defensive attitude where focusing on a single interest becomes the only way to avoid losing control. On the other hand is the desire to advance with simple prototyping and believing that rolling out ever new quick solutions is the best way to solve the issue. The development journey for both is to recognize the importance of the opposing perspective and to build on one's strength rather than falling back into the shadow side of it. Figure 4.2 offers a visual representation of the polarity switch of C and D.

Facilitators of stakeholder processes face of course other issues as well. The most common challenges that we can attribute to the group level of such processes concerns the strength polarity of those seeking Efficacy at all cost and those wishing to ensure that resources are adequately shared so that everybody can contribute and also benefit from the project. Efficacy-focused group members understand the value of having those with certain expertise focus on certain tasks rather than spending too much time teaching other new skills. When pushed, such members can advocate a specialization of the whole project in such a way that silos prevent a collaboration across thematic sub-projects, leading to a loss of synergy among the various work streams. Those members who favor sharing as a underlying value, will advocate that nobody can be left behind and that resources must be equally split, rather than allocated among those members best fit to complete a task. When pushed by those who prefer an effective way of advancing, members with a preference for sharing might fall back into a stance where they become very focused on securing their own rights and resource access, not wanting to lose out and becoming very protective of sub-groups that may be perceived

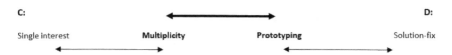

Figure 4.2 The polarity switch of two opposing limitations into a strength polarity

as losing out when resources are allocated. Here the developmental journeys consist of understanding and embracing both opposing strengths and finding solutions that are both efficient and take into account the importance of sharing insights and ideas with those less obviously equipped to provide input (see Figure 4.3).

Collective solutions unfold when the participating groups embrace their superpowers

Interviews with Collaboratory practitioners, insights from literature, as well as our own experience suggest that the developmental challenge at the group level is to achieve collective solutions. This requires integrating the two competing strengths outlined in Figure 4.4.

When group-level strength polarities turn into limitations, these are much easier to be detected and picked up than the individual polarities discussed in the previous chapter. They tend to take up space and shake the process. This is where facilitation skills come into play. In the earlier example, process experience and solid judgment will be required to decide if it is best to continue or amend an anticipated process step at a given time. Such integration requires a group dynamics that honor the benefits of analyzing the underlying cause and consequence of an issue, and ensures a shared understanding that developing breakthrough solutions requires letting go of the problem and starting from an ideal future vision. In the same way we offered pathways to advance toward such an integration at the individual level, we would like to outline three underlying strength polarities at the group level. These three pairs are less proven truths and more abstractions that can be used as signposts on the integration journey.

Figure 4.3 The polarity switch of two opposing limitations into a strength polarity

Figure 4.4 The strength polarities and superpowers at the group level

A Deep Search arises from analysis and vision, letting go of the problem and the dream

The first strength polarity is about getting the best out of the desire of **Analysis**, as well as **Envisioning** a dream on which to build new solutions. In such an integration, the benefits of the analytical capacity are transformed to contribute to common search methodologies that provide scientific rigor to emerging processes. The challenge herein lies in the ability to apply a problem analysis capacity to finding scientific means to measure the validity of real-time emerging solutions. This implies transforming the traditional problem-based scientific mind to scientific methodologies such as Deep Search which are able to provide scientific support in the sense-making journey of back-casting exercises to define prototyping and piloting processes. In the same logic, the strength of visioning new ideals is challenged to ensure that emerging collective visions are translated into actionable solutions. This challenge includes the necessity to materialize ideal dreams into a series of concrete prototypes that can be tested against a series of limitations and constraints that relate to the existing underlying symptoms of the problem. Analytical skills and competencies allow substantiating prototype ideas to protect against unintended negative consequences. When combined, these competing strengths become the Deep Search superpower and make collective solutions possible and prosperous (see Figure 4.5).

The initial Collaboratory book, which was written by seasoned practitioners of co-creative multi-stakeholder processes, provides an extensive overview of the complexity of these two competing strengths. On the one hand, Deep Search with its ability to shift from data analysis to observing real-time progress is an essential tool for providing scientific support to prototyping and piloting work. Such rigor is most essential and yet very difficult to develop in such explorative and complex processes. On the other hand, the ability to embrace a collective ideal vision requires moving beyond a single stakeholder perspective. Unless we are able to create space to tap into the group consciousness, stakeholders will keep debating potential solutions only from each of their perspectives. The Collaboratory work we have conducted both before and after the Collaboratory book has confirmed the centrality of integrating these two competing strengths and the need to overcome the limitations of both along the way.

Figure 4.5 From strength polarity to Superpower

Collaboration results from prototyping, multiplicity beyond single interest and quick solutions

The second strength polarity addresses the dimension of Multiplicity versus Prototyping. Embracing **Multiplicity** consists of the challenge of allowing complex interdependences while acknowledging the various different interests. In a group setting, this is reflected in the developmental challenge of listening to contradicting opinions, moving beyond black and white worldviews and single interests. It is about overcoming the perspective of single interest to appreciating competing systems. The challenge here is not just to agree that there are different points of view, but also to look beyond different perspectives and identify potentially competing systems. These include competing values, competing definitions of success, competing approaches to building solutions, and competing ways of providing support. The ability for such a broader subjectivity is one of the two competing strengths at this level. We call the ability of contributing to such a space the strength of Multiplicity. **Prototyping**, on the other hand, is a strength that consists of the developmental challenge of wanting new solutions quickly and being patient enough to properly prototype them. In order words, the ability of combining a playful attitude of wanting to find solutions at any price, with the courage of testing these emerging solutions with others in a concrete way. When we manage to see and accept **Multiplicity** and have a capacity and appetite to **Prototype**, the shift toward a **Collaboration** is in sight. Figure 4.6 illustrates this.

This strength polarity is supported by interviews and research. We have come to differentiate the two as different types of collaboration. In terms of managing multiplicity, the challenge of being able to move beyond ignoring systemic consequences to embracing contradictions has been defined as the developmental journey of complex interdependencies. Allowing for multiplicity is critical to ensure that naïve solutions are tested against undesired negative consequences that further aggravate the problem or create a new one. Social innovators often joke that most of our current problems have been caused by previous attempts at fixing other problems. In the literature, this strength polarity of multiplicity and prototyping includes levels of development and group coherence. Graves suggests that the challenge of moving from a single system view to multiple competing systems as advancing levels

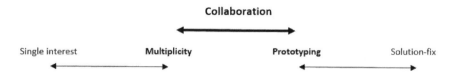

Figure 4.6 From strength polarity to Superpower

of development. Single subjectivity can hence develop into a so-called relativistic perspective of challenges. In Collaboratories we have observed, shifting from a single system view to embracing multiple competing systems is indeed a key transformative moment. The idea of Prototyping is central to our Collaboratory research and involves the shift of moving from known solutions to daring to co-create new solutions by building new prototypes and pilots. Research highlights the challenge of acknowledging that it may take more than the existing solutions to solve the wicked problems that Collaboratories are seeking to solve. This capacity requires an ability, willingness, and space of co-creation and moving beyond what is known.

Mastery combines efficacy with sharing, overcoming a need for protection or specialization

The third underlying strength polarity in the journey toward collective solutions at the group level is efficacy and sharing. **Efficacy** in itself holds the challenge of overcoming the need to fall back on specialization as a solution for efficiency. This includes appreciating the multiple ways of defining what may be efficient for a team, a project, or a process, and actively embracing the multiple dimensions that contribute to efficacy. For group processes, this strength is invaluable and an advanced competency. The challenge here is to achieve a collective solution that arises through inclusion rather than competing or specializing. The challenge here lies in recognizing the benefit of learning together rather than specializing in what we know already and working in silos. **Sharing** consists of the ability of sharing available resources. In a world where resources are perceived as being limited, both in our heads and in a real sense, it is not easy to trust that there is enough time, space, money, people, ideas, support, and encouragement for what this project and this group may need. It really challenges each stakeholder group to move beyond the need of first protecting resources for what they view most important to taking a more generous perspective saying, "There is enough for all of us." When we integrate both strengths, we can see how they can play together and build the understanding to allocate available resources in the best interest of the project and competing interests. The beauty of integrating a broader sense of multiplicity and a true sense of generosity to share, again, brings a multi-stakeholder group a big step forward in engaging in truly collective solutions along with potentially conflicting fellow stakeholders. Mastery occurs when a new core process or competence was acquired together. The challenge here lies in taking the time rather than taking a short-cut. When we look beyond the challenges contained in reaching the two individual strengths, there is true beauty emerging from the integration of both efficacy and sharing. Imagine a group that is able to be Appreciative of different ways of achieving a shared vision and solution, taking the time for those select few competencies or processes are must be acquired together in order to advance as a whole.

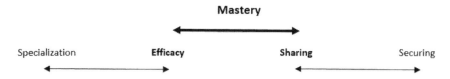

Figure 4.7 From strength polarity to Superpower

The two strengths are truly opposing and can easily cancel each other out. Efficiency claims can prevent a generous attempt of sharing and prioritizing shared learning may kill efficacy. As outlined in Figure 4.7, being able to overcome these limitations and to integrate both strengths into the Mastery superpower brings a group closer to collective solutions.

Graves's levels of development and Wilson's perspective of sociobiology help us further understand the underlying challenges in this strength polarity. Graves calls this level "strategic" and describes the journey as moving from ideology and objective control to multiplicity and therefore efficacy. Such a strategic approach to solving a problem is often highlighted as a key hurdle in group processes. Wilson's work on competition looks at shifting a group behavior from being self-serving and protecting sub-group interests. He explains the challenge of letting go of a sense of self-protection and daring to embrace sharing with others, pointing out how complex and multidimensional it is for a group to shift toward Mastery. Huh has studied group coherence and the importance of being altruistic. He explains the ability to share resources and expressing altruism as a shift from self-destruction or guilt. Sharing is as an important factor to move beyond focusing on the real limitations that exist in any project to develop the required group coherence to succeed.

Deep Search, Collaboration, and Mastery are the superpowers for collective solutions

The strength polarities are all elements that create the enabling superpowers so that groups of people and organizations of all kind can truly work together and advance toward the collective solution of a problem a multi-stakeholder group wishes to solve.

The superpower in each of the three levels are described in Figure 4.8. The strength duo analysis versus vision can be integrated into a state called **Deep Search**. Deep Search symbolizes an applied scientific mind in a future-oriented journey and requires the analytical mind to find ways to support solution development with rigor. The strength pair multiplicity versus prototyping can be augmented into a superpower called **Collaboration**. Collaboration is

all about taking into account interdependencies when co-creating and test-ing new prototype solutions. The strength polarity of efficacy and sharing can be integrated into the superpower called **Mastery**. Embracing the fact that we are all on an inclusive, common journey toward a new solution is the ultimate ingredient for a successful multi-stakeholder process. It requires the understanding that there is no single right way to a successful end goal. It also implies that a group achieves efficacy when no expert group works in isolation, and mixed competency groups work and learn with each other. Figure 4.9 is a visual way of showing the superpowers.

Group level:

COLLECTIVE SOLUTIONS

Strength polarity		Super power
Analysis	Vision	**Deep Search**
Complexity	Prototyping	**Collaboration**
Efficacy	Sharing	**Mastery**

Figure 4.8 Overview of group level strength polarities and superpowers

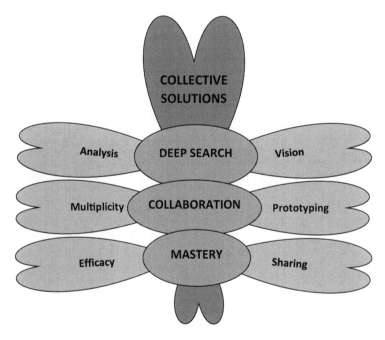

Figure 4.9 Visual overview of group level strength polarities and superpowers

Summary

- Insights from participants and relevant literature, as well as from Collaboratory facilitators, have identified a number of pathways to ensure group effectiveness in a multi-stakeholder co-creation process. These pathways have to do with both translating limiting behaviors into their original strengths and then with integrating competing strength polarities into a superpower.
- The overarching strength polarity for groups is about integrating Analysis of the symptoms and the Vision of new ideals. Underneath these are other polarities that can be used as pathways to achieving Collective Solutions for the problem the group has agreed to get together to solve.
- The strength called "Analysis" relates to the strengths Multiplicity and Efficacy.
- The strength called "Vision" is bundled with other strengths such as Prototyping and Sharing.
- Each strength polarity can ideally be integrated into a superpower, and requires having looked at the blind spots of the limiting expressions of underlying strengths.

Reflection questions

- Refer to Figure 4.4 and imagine on which of the two sides you have more likely your strength when representing your organization or an initiative about which you deeply care. Ask yourself the following two questions to know where to place the **circle** on each of the four lines:
  - First ask yourself: which strength is more dominant in me (left or right side)?
  - Then ask yourself: do I live the circled strength more as a positive or a limiting expression (which side of the vertical line within a strength polarity: toward the center for a positive expression, toward the outside for a limiting expression)?

Repeat this for the other levels.

- Using the same Figures 4.5, 4.6, and 4.7, imagine what happens when adversity strikes and you get pushed into a corner. Most likely you will find yourself on the outer right or left sides of the vertical line. Place a **cross** at the point of the limitations you see yourself expressing more naturally. You could find yourself either on the same strength as above on the opposite side.

Repeat this for the other levels.

- Look at what picture presents itself across all the four levels. What emerges for you and what learnings and insights can you generate for

yourself? How could you help others in your team when several of you represent a particular stakeholder interest?

- If you are currently actively participating in a co-creative multi-stakeholder process, here are some useful questions to ask yourself about each of the four levels:

  - What progress have I observed so far?
  - What further potential do I see?
  - What can I concretely do or be to bring about this potential?
  - What change do I commit to applaud and celebrate when it will occur?

Further reading and references

Graves, C.W. (1970): Levels of existence: An open system theory of values. *Journal of Humanistic Psychology* Vol 10 No 2, 131–155.

Huh, Yeol, Reigeluth, Charles M., & Lee, Dabae (2014): Collective efficacy and its relationship with leadership in a computer-mediated project-based group work. *Contemporary Educational Technology* Vol 1 No 5, 1–21.

Muff, Katrin (ed.) (2014): *The Collaboratory – a co-creative stakeholder engagement process for solving complex issues.* Greenleaf Publishing, Sheffield.

Wilson, David S. (2007): Rethinking the theoretical foundation of sociobiology. *The Quarterly Review of Biology* Vol 82 No 4, 327–348.

Group level:

Please take a moment to reflect on your personal strengths and experiences that can serve you in this domain of change.

Appreciation

Please take a moment to reflect on your personal strengths and experiences that can serve you in this domain of change.

Superpower #3 – transformative spaces of facilitators

The challenge in holding the space for a shared issue is being too strict or lost in facilitation

Facilitators face different challenges, particularly when they work in teams. We have experienced a situation whereby one of the facilitators was in charge of defining an ideal process and leading the innovation day accordingly, and the other facilitator had the role of paying attention to what was happening in the room and adapting to what was emerging and amending the process as a result. While I have witnessed many great such co-creation days, this one didn't go so well and ended up tearing up the process. Things got messed up when, after lunchtime, five new stakeholders showed up – late.

One of the facilitators, the "adapter," happily brought the latecomers into the process and suggested a modification of the first exercise in the afternoon. The other facilitator, the "structured," rolled his eyes in despair. He knew that this was going to knock off the momentum he had managed to create in the morning and which the team needed to build on to advance. He was mad that the latecomers came in seemingly unconscious of their delay and with no apology. As soon as the "adapter" had completed a short introductory round, the "structured" facilitator jumped in and took over to bring the process back on track. He changed the initial exercise he had planned and allocated the newcomers equally into five existing groups and gave everybody a brainstorming task to complete. The "adapter" looked at him as if he had lost his mind. As soon as the participants had split into the various groups, the two of them got together in a corner. Each accused the other of disrupting their efforts. Their attention was no longer with the group and they were unable to do what facilitators are meant to do: to hold a space for participants to advance in a project together. The energy in the room

had changed and the momentum was lost. It would have taken the full attention of both facilitators to ensure that the newcomers integrated well into the teams and yet their attention was elsewhere. But not only the two facilitators failed to adapt to the new situation, but so did the existing participants. After the next break, a number of participants had strolled off claiming to have to tend to urgent matters and the group was at a point of disintegrating.

Let us look at what happened to the shared issue space here when two facilitators were unable to coordinate their different ideas about how to integrate latecomers. Let's remember that there is no right and wrong and that these examples serve to illustrate delicate points that can create a process breakdown. Table 5.1 describes the two perspectives of the two facilitators:

These two perspectives originate in two strengths. It is the care for structure on the one hand, and the care for flexibility and adaptability on the other hand that have created this conflict between the two. When any strength is over-expressed, it can easily be perceived as a threat and become a limitation to the process. How can the knowledge and experience of carefully designing transformative spaces for multi-stakeholders through structured spaces be augmented by the skills and competencies of playing with what is happening in the room and adapting the carefully designed plan to achieve an even better outcome for the group?

- **A:** The "structured" brings the strength of anticipating various scenarios of how to advance a group of individuals and stakeholders from one point in the process to the next. This strength can turn into a limitation when he rejects change or new members showing up and becomes strictly attached to his agenda and insists that only he knows how to proceed.
- **B:** The "adapter" has a strength of not being attached to a set agenda with a focus on what is happening in the room and ready and willing to adapt

Table 5.1 First example of opposing limitations at the shared issue level

1st example of opposing polarities emerging at the shared issue level:	
I A: The process was well planned and we had agreed what to do. How can we accept new members in who will totally disrupt the great momentum we have built?	B: We need to play with what we have and go with the flow. How can you interrupt me when I improvise and try to save the situation? It is my job to adopt the process, not yours!

to what is emerging, including new people showing up. In his creativity of being playful to what emerges, his strength can turn into a limitation whereby he will be closed to the idea of sticking with the original plan. Something new popped up and he totally trusts it will work out, possibly throwing the baby out with the bathwater.

When both limitations are facing each other, then a conflict is nearly unavoidable. The "structured" facilitator will become strict and possibly inflexible, insisting on knowing how to proceed, while the "adapter" will close down and retreat from the discussion. It will be challenging for both to find a common language to deal with the situation, which is a loss for the process as it is now a gamble whose process preference will be used and if that was the right call. When both facilitators are able to step back from caring so much about their preferred reaction to a challenging situation and can see how both perspectives can add value in a complex situation, it may be able to find back to a dialogue. We all have a bit of both strengths anchored in us and it is interesting to note which one is dominant in what situations and to what degree that is truly in the best interest of the space we are holding. Figure 5.1 illustrates the two strengths and their limitations.

There are, of course, other ways that processes break down when looking at what happens at the common space of the shared issue. Facilitation can be handled by a single person or by a pair of facilitators. Both have their challenges. When facilitating alone, I make sure I spend time reflecting on what is needed from an energy level for the group process. One of the challenges that I have faced was the hard decision on when a group needs harmony to advance and when a bit of a productive tension can create a breakthrough. Getting this balance right is an art not a science and depends really on one best gut feeling. While experience helps, being able to ask oneself the right questions is also helpful. Overstretching the sense of wanting to create harmony can go as far as creating a dissonance with what is actually happening in the room. Imagine somebody ignoring an important tension in the room and suggesting an exercise that artificially tries to generate a sense of harmony. Depending on the energy in the room and among the various members in the groups, this can blow up in a very unharmonious way. I have learned never to ignore an unpleasant tension and to think very carefully about how to address it, rather than to hope it would pass. Alternatively, when a conflict or tension is not yet ripe to be discussed in a way that can generate a potential

Figure 5.1 The polarity switch of two opposing limitations into a strength polarity

Dissonance   **Harmony**   **Breakthrough**   Breakdown

Figure 5.2 The polarity switch of two opposing limitations into a strength polarity

positive breakthrough, pushing for an open discussion of a conflict or tension between parties or different perspectives can result in a breakdown of the discussion and put the process a few steps back. This requires an important skill of a facilitator, the ability to hold tensions and to hold them lightly enough to find ways to dance around them, while knowing when to step in and address them. Figure 5.2 illustrates the two limitations and their associated strengths.

When looking at the challenges of how to ensure an effective space of co-creation throughout a co-creation process, facilitators have reported a number of limiting issues that can cause a process disruption. Let us look at another example from the perspective of opposing limitations that we will subsequently turn into strength polarities.

A similarly challenged situation occurred in another Collaboratory setting. Two very skilled facilitators worked together and were both aware of an approaching breakthrough moment for the group. It had been a rough weekend and both were eager to ensure the group could walk away with the results they so desperately needed. The energy was high and the room over-heated. The "stillness" facilitator felt it was high time for a moment of personal reflection and without verifying with her colleague ended a group exercise with the calm invitation that everybody should find a comfortable space to sit down and reflect on what has been a most important lesson learned in the past two days. The "connector" saw the energy of the room collapse and half of the people disengage. She observed how some grabbed their phones and started texting. For her this situation became an emergency: if they wanted to succeed with their weekend objective, they couldn't let the room deflate and the people switch off. It was now or never. So, after less than two minutes of silence, she cheerfully clapped in her hands. She announced with a chirpy voice that those who felt more inclined to engage in a conversation with somebody rather than reflecting by themselves should connect to another participant and engage in the following question: "Tell me something entirely new – even mind-blowing – about what you think would make this project really fly." The "stillness" facilitator was stunned to silence. She couldn't believe what just happened. Her

colleague facilitator had stepped into a beautiful emerging silence that could have been a key to create important progress to suggest the very opposite of an exercise that now entirely ruined the space for those who had started to reflect. She felt the energy was gone. She was confused and stepped out of the room. The "connector" sensed that something was wrong but felt too overloaded with the quickly changing energy in the room and the need to answer questions about how to meet whom and when to be back, that she couldn't also handle her obviously distressed co-facilitator. It was all too much and things were really not working out. The participants were also confused and indeed the intense energy in the room just became nervous and distracting.

This is a scenario that can happen when two well-meaning and experienced facilitators have different intuitions about a given situation and cannot find a space to synchronize. Often such dances work out well, but sometimes they don't. Table 5.2 summarizes the two limiting expressions of strengths illustrated above.

These limitations reflect real situations we have experienced in Collaboratory situations. The trick here is to focus on each of the underlying strengths that is hidden underneath these opposing limitations.

- **C:** The "stillness" facilitator brings the strength of sensing when a group needs a space for reflection to make a next important step forward. She can sense the energy and when it is so full with busy chatter that nothing new can happen. This strength turns into a limitation when things don't happen as quietly and well organized as she imagines and when she gets lost, she might feel disoriented and will herself need a moment of quiet to find her own center again.
- **D:** The "connector" has a strength of daring to challenge the group to share and to be exposed to an entirely new idea with the hope to blow their minds. This strength can turn into a limitation when impatience gets the better of her and silence stresses her out to the point that she feels

Table 5.2 Second example of opposing limitations at the shared issue level

2nd example of opposing polarities emerging at the shared issue level:	
2 C: It is in silence, in deeper reflection and in slowing down that we can find groundbreaking new solutions. We must have space and time.	D: Inspiration doesn't happen in listening to oneself think, it happens when engaging with others and being exposed to new ideas.

Figure 5.3 The polarity switch of two opposing limitations into a strength polarity

people are disengaging. She will actually stop sensing what is happening when she gets overloaded with unexpected questions of an intervention she maybe did not entirely carefully plan, and she may lose her red thread in the course.

Figure 5.3 shows the transfer from a limitation to a strength in the second story and for the examples C and D. When wanting to impose stillness, the result can be an agitation in the room by those who are not ready for the stillness. And when seeking to create a connection becomes too much enforced, the result can be that the group fragments or breaks apart. Knowing what to offer as a productive space and when, is a challenge and while it often helps to have two facilitators to better sense what might be needed, sometimes two opinions can ruin a beautiful process, too. By matching these two strengths and by pairing them into polarities, we acknowledge that they are competing.

When the two strengths enrich each other, a superpower of performance can be attained. This is the overarching challenge that facilitators face when embracing the task of enabling a group of stakeholders to advance toward a transformative spaces.

Transformative spaces emerge when the common space of a shared issue is full of superpowers

The strength polarities provide insights into the pathways of holding a space and creating transformation. Integrating these polarities enables the ideal state of facilitation, which is all about creating the right energy in the room (see Figure 5.4).

Awareness enables an adaptive structure that is neither too strict nor disconnected

The capability to be **Structured** consists of the ability of consciously facilitating powerful spaces of transformation. The journey for this strength is to overcome the limitation to be too strict on what was planned to being able to maintain one's focus on what is important while being able to step back to see the larger picture. Creating spaces for transformation seeks to touch the

individual and the group. Designing such a process that touches upon these elements when needed is an art that is best learned through practice. Such practice results in an increasing degree of consciousness about what happens at the various levels of transformation and how these interact. The capacity to be **Adaptive**, on the other hand, relates to sensing how to give time for what is needed to happen without planning for it ahead of time. The journey here is to shift from closing down at some point and not wanting to hear new ideas anymore to finding new energy and space for bringing new ideas and new members on board if and when needed. Such an ability demands being able to be truly in the present moment at the service of what is happening and emerging right now (see Figure 5.5).

The strength polarity was developed by listening to the experience of facilitators of stakeholder co-created processes, the collective experience of people who are working with the Collaboratory methodology specifically. This polarity is relatively easily accessible to new facilitators and is obvious to discuss in a post-reflection after a facilitation supervision. This is also an art that is best acquired through practice and through expanding one's capacity for mindfulness. A skilled facilitator is able to integrate these strengths, can both plan the interventions that are needed and be able to be adaptive to what is needed, and as a result, move the group toward transformative spaces. Both of the preceding examples are two polarities with the potential of breaking down a process, or how their successful integration can help create the magic that makes such complex processes fly. The related superpower creates magic and self-confidence in the facilitator.

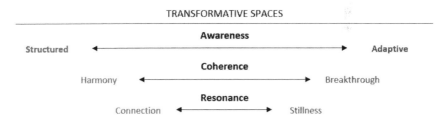

Figure 5.4 The strength polarities and superpowers at the shared issue level

Figure 5.5 From strength polarity to Superpower

Coherence is the ideal of breakthrough and harmony, avoiding breakdown and dissonance

The strength polarity compares the idea of harmony and the benefit of break-through. **Harmony** is the result of a process of achieving a better alignment among stakeholders. The developmental journey of shifting from conflict and dissonance in a group to a sense of alignment is often painful but invaluable for bringing out the best in the group. Conflicts originally have to do with rejecting new ideas and other opinions and can result in a process to become lame. Experience indicates that stakeholders work better together when they are aligned and in harmony with each other. They can co-create more power-fully. Learning how to achieve such a coherence without forcing a consensus is part of a facilitator's skillset. On the other hand, **Breakthrough** in itself holds the developmental range of being able to break down processes in the worst case to driving positive change with true breakthrough. There are ways to engineer such positive change through framing and facilitation. There are co-creative group processes that foster breakthrough ideas more than others do and a facilitator can build these in. Breakthroughs remain breakthroughs and are not entirely predictable and tensions arise when there is something cooking that is at odds with the planning process of the facilitator. These skills of creating harmony amongst stakeholders and the skill of allowing breakthroughs to destroy such harmony are both obvious. Being able to inte-grate both of them with the intention of creating a space where a disruption can augment the current level of coherence is a true superpower reserved for the truly brave. It is a key enabler toward creating transformative spaces (see Figure 5.6).

In the literature, Bushe and his colleagues in organizational change suggest that synergy is achieved when the conflict and dissonance can be transformed into alignment and high coherence. They point out the value of achieving such a shift for a group in a change process and suggest that high coherence requires having overcome dissonance. Alan Watkins who has studied what it takes to achieve new breakthroughs points to the need of chaos that can cause process breakdowns as a basis for creating disruption through new kinds of ideas, which in themselves are also disruptive – however in a positive way by generating breakthrough insights. The opposition of these strengths is a great insight in a facilitation process.

Figure 5.6 From strength polarity to Superpower

Resonance occurs in moments of stillness and connection, overcoming agitation and fragmentation

The third strength polarity involves silent spaces and connections. **Stillness** is about the power of self-reflection in order to transform beliefs and convictions into openness to what might be. The development journey is to shift from busy chatter that pretends to be productive to slowing down into doing nothing for a moment. My key insight from years of Collaboratory work is that deep transformation only happens in moments of silence. For things to click with ourselves or among ourselves, any sound or movement might be a distraction. A facilitator will ensure to create stillness to enable the complex process of transformation at the individual and group levels, both by planning them in and by creating them when a breakthrough moment has approached. **Connections**, on the other hand, bring power and strength to co-creative solutions. They contain the challenge of finding space in one's overloaded and pre-occupied mind to connect and listen to a stranger or to strange ideas. A facilitator carefully weights how to shift from moments where a group may feel overloaded and overwhelmed to moments where anybody who is willing to listen carefully can be blown-away by a new idea from somebody with whom they have not yet truly engaged. Transformation is triggered by new ideas and not by an overloaded mind. Integrating both strengths consists of designing spaces and times that counter-balance the sense of being lost and overwhelmed in the thick of intense project and teamwork. It is about using moments of stillness and connection as acupuncture points for change (see Figure 5.7).

This polarity is very much inspired by reflections among colleague Collaboratory practitioners. Our combined Collaboratory experience has demonstrated the importance of creating moments of reflection and of silence, and has made us understand that it is mostly in silence and being still that we can sense that deeper resonance with others and new insights can shift us into a next phase of transformation. Listen to oneself is matched by the need to listen to others. The journey around reflection has to do with getting lost in thoughts and too much information to embracing the power of silent spaces of reflection. The journey of listening involves also overcoming moments of information overflow to creating a space in one's head and heart to have new conversations with strangers and truly listen to different perspectives and insights they bring.

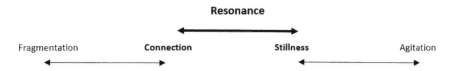

Figure 5.7 From strength polarity to Superpower

Awareness, Coherence, and Resonance are superpowers for transformative spaces

The superpower in each of the four levels is described in Figure 5.8. Here we are talking about superpowers that relate to the space, the energy in the room, that serve to advance the issue that is to be resolved. These superpowers thus reside more in the energetic domain than as competencies of a single person or a facilitator. A facilitator will attain them by mastering the underlying strengths so that she will have acquired a fluency to shift between both, sensing what is most required in a given moment of time to enable the group to reach a next stage in their journey together.

When structure is able to support adaptation, the energy in the room can be described as an **Awareness**. A facilitator can connect to this and sense what is needed next. When harmony and breakthrough are perfectly well supporting each other, we talk about a **Coherence**. In such moment, the space is open and receptive, fully aware that whatever insight comes next will disrupt everything that was so far and transform the common space into a next level of a newly found coherence. Imagine a situation where people are so connected with each other and the issue they work on, that they can embrace stillness and dive into silence together, sensing that something much deeper may emerge that words could never capture. The energy in the room in such a situation is best described as a **Resonance** and it is palpable for any person in the room. Facilitators can sense these superpowers and will experience these magic moments where they are more guided than choosing willfully themselves what is required next. Athletes talk about flow and the state that occurs is a physical or embodied experience that happens when all inner systems – blood circulation, nerves, brain activity, and more sync in alignment with the largest engine in the human body, the heart rhythm. You can train to be in that state and that is a useful practice for facilitators. The science behind this discovery is called HeartMath (reference follows). Figure 5.9 is a visual way of showing the superpowers.

Shared issue level:

TRANSFORMATIVE SPACES

Strength polarity		Super power
Structured	Adaptive	**Awareness**
Harmony	Breakthrough	**Coherence**
Connection	Stillness	**Resonance**

Figure 5.8 Overview of space level strength polarities and superpowers

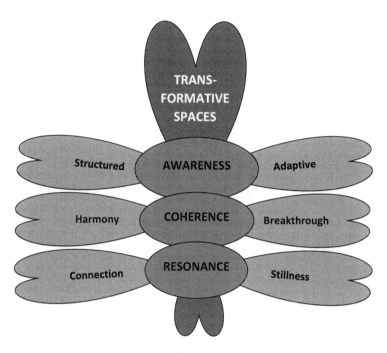

Figure 5.9 Visual overview of space level strength polarities and superpowers

Summary

- We have gathered insights from facilitators and change experts around the world to identify relevant pathways toward transformative spaces among multi-stakeholders. These pathways are all about translating limiting attitudes into their original strengths and then with integrating competing strength polarities into a superpower.
- The overarching strength polarity for the shared issue is about integrating a structured space and an adaptive space. Underneath, these are three more subtle levels of polarities that can be used as pathways for creating a shared issue for the project and its solution through transformative spaces among a changing group of stakeholders.
- A structured space has other developmental strengths that relate to it including a high coherence and heart-connection, as well as on a more subtle level, silent spaces.
- An adaptive space is connected to strengths such as disruptive ideas and new skills, and at a more subtle level, new conversations.
- Each strength polarity can ideally be integrated into a superpower, and requires having looked at the blind spots of the limiting expressions of underlying strengths.

Reflection questions

- Refer to Figure 5.4 and imagine on which of the two sides you more likely have your strengths when facilitating a meeting of stakeholders. Ask yourself the following two questions to know where to place the **circle** on each of the four lines:

  - First ask yourself: which strength is more dominant in me (left or right side)?
  - Then ask yourself: do I live the circled strength more as a positive or a limiting expression (which side of the vertical line within a strength polarity: toward the center for a positive expression, toward the outside for a limiting expression)?

Repeat this for the other levels.

- Using the same Figures 5.5, 5.6, and 5.7, imagine what happens when adversity strikes and you get pushed into a corner. Most likely you will find yourself on the outer right or left sides of the vertical line. Place a **cross** at the point of the limitations you see yourself expressing more naturally. You could find yourself either on the same strength as above on the opposite side.

Repeat this for the other levels.

- Look at what picture presents itself across all the four levels. What emerges for you and what learnings and insights can you generate for yourself? How could you help others in your team when several of you represent a particular stakeholder interest?
- If you are currently facilitating a co-creative multi-stakeholder process, here are some useful questions to ask yourself about each of the four levels:

  - What is my one personal limitation here?
  - What are my two key personal strengths here?
  - What is the one best way for me to call out limitations and ask the group to enable all of us to move beyond my limitations?
  - What is the one inspiring comment to alert the group that I will hold our space when things get tough?

Further reading and references

Bushe, Gervase R., & Marshak, Robert J. (2015): The dialogic mindset in organization development. The dialogic mindset in organization development. *Research in Organizational Change and Development* Vol 22, 55–97.

HeartMath: www.heartmath.com/ accessed March 30, 2018.

Muff, Katrin (ed.) (2014): *The Collaboratory – a co-creative stakeholder engagement process for solving complex issues.* Greenleaf Publishing, Sheffield.

Watkins, Alan, & Wilber, Ken (2015): *Wicked and wise – how to solve the world's toughest problems.* Urban Publishing, Croydon.

Shared issue level:

Please take a moment to reflect on your personal strengths and experiences that can serve you in this domain of change.

Focus

Please take a moment to reflect on your personal strengths and experiences that can serve you in this domain of change.

Part III

Co-creation for change makers

There are three key ingredients for a successful stakeholder co-creation: change makers, process building blocks, and process measurement. Experience has shown that the relational dimension of a project involving stakeholders is a key factor of success or failure. We offer here a unique way to measure how the process is doing, not the actual outcome of it, but the process itself. We uncover blind spots that can slow down or sabotage a process. Such a measurement comes as a necessary addition to existing project measurement tools that assess critical path items and outcomes.

Chapter 6 focuses on the key ingredient of any successful transformation: the change maker. You will meet you will meet seven change makers from all walks of life: **Christoph** *holds an executive position in an international organization. He is struggling how to align his values with the priorities of the business.* **Claudine** *is a freelance trainer in her early fifties and her challenge is to translate her love for learning into valuable business propositions.* **Eleanor** *is a teacher at a business school in her mid-fifties, challenged to adapt her teaching style to the demands of a changing world.* **Jannick** *is an idealist at heart in his mid-thirties with a burning desire to make a difference. He wants to set up his consulting company.* **Marianne** *is an innovative dean in a business school who is wondering how to go about transforming business education.* **Max** *works in a purpose-driven institution and co-leads an important initiative that brings together projects and organizations that work on solving a burning issue.* **Simone** *is a program director for professional development.*

Chapter 7 outlines the building blocks for a successful multi-stakeholder co-creation process. The roles of the initiator and the facilitator are studied in more detail given their importance for the process. We clarify the difference between the short and the long innovation cycles and identify key activities and achievements in each step.

Chapter 8 provides an answer to the need to be able to measure progress in the process of co-creation rather than only measuring productive outcomes. Measuring the invisible is a challenge and this chapter highlights the development challenges for the initiator, participants, and the facilitator across the building blocks of the process. The Competency Assessment of Responsible Leadership (CARL) serves to measure the progress of individual players in terms of competencies at specific steps of the process.

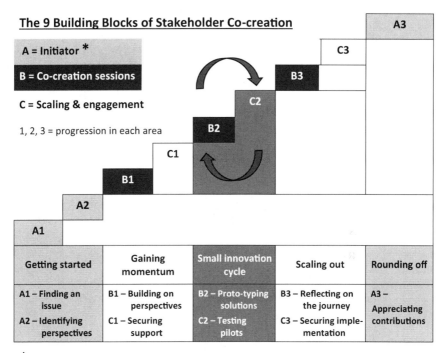

The 9 Building Blocks of Stakeholder Co-creation

A = Initiator *

B = Co-creation sessions

C = Scaling & engagement

1, 2, 3 = progression in each area

Getting started	Gaining momentum	Small innovation cycle	Scaling out	Rounding off
A1 – Finding an issue	B1 – Building on perspectives	B2 – Proto-typing solutions	B3 – Reflecting on the journey	A3 – Appreciating contributions
A2 – Identifying perspectives	C1 – Securing support	C2 – Testing pilots	C3 – Securing implementation	

* A change maker or an organization

Figure III.1 The essential building blocks of co-creation

If there was one image that could summarize key insights in Part III – beyond the fact that there is a change maker in you for sure! – it would be Figure III.1. *What this image seeks to illustrate is that co-creation processes consist of individual steps that can be built together into tailor-made processes of change in service of whatever great idea you are trying to realize. While the entire process is one big process of innovation, experience has shown that in the middle of the process, there is a small innovation cycle. We also know that the process consists of meetings (sessions or events) and a lot of work in between that is typically undervalued and underestimated. Furthermore, particular attention is placed on the role and journey of the initiator. An initiator may be an individual change maker or an organization in search of the next great thing. Without the specific steps of the initiator, co-creation processes are highly sensitive to failure and time has taught us to greatly value these steps, both before and after the "real" process.*

The different types and roles of change makers

There is a change maker either in you or near you; they all greatly care for the world

Claudine is a trainer and coach. She runs her own business, teaches on the side at a business school, and is the in-house coach for a couple of long-standing clients. She understands that the reality is very dynamic, and she has adapted her offer and her business model nearly every year over the past six, seven years as she looks back and she learns new emerging models. While this is exciting, it is also tiring. Developing a new business model is never easy. It needs to be tested and adapted, and sometimes she feels she's doing more talking than working. Partnerships have become fluid and changing, and she has learned some hard lessons about how collaboration needs to become much more flexible around issues such as ownership and decision-making models. She is curious about new organizational forms. She loves the idea of self-organizing, but she also understands that without hierarchy, work does not necessarily happen. She has experienced firsthand how relationships can otherwise be affected, and even be destroyed.

Claudine is in her 50s, comfortably so. Her kids are in the middle of their life journeys, and she feels she is in a good place, having been able to let go of wanting to steer their lives into preset directions, as she feels her parents have attempted to do with her. She is a bit overwhelmed with how much there is to continuously learn, and while she is eager to keep on developing her competencies and skills, she's also wondering how she can translate what she learns into chargeable services that she as a facilitator and learning enabler can offer to her business clients. Increasingly, she works also with social entrepreneurs, small companies. She helps them to make sense of how to organize around their desire to develop, to realize, a new idea that unites them. There is not much

money to be made with social enterprise startups, but she loves the energy that oozes in these places and is more than willing to give back at very reduced fees to enable these startups to get off the ground. She does know that working for free doesn't work, and that her work must be valued and appreciated so that she can actually get the key players to engage. She wonders, with many of the interesting initiatives that are up for grabs: how much free upfront work is healthy and necessary, and when she can insist on getting paid a fair price for what she offers.

We are using a program designed to help change makers develop in their journey as backdrop for telling the story of how our seven change makers address their personal and professional challenges to advance in their individual learning journeys to become more fluent in leading and co-creating change. The program is called Impact Leadership Program (or ILP) and is a one-year part-time continuous education program that aims at development of future-relevant leadership competencies, helping organizations to sustain in the *volatile, uncertain, complex,* and *ambiguous* (VUCA) world. We shall use the program to provide the context to illustrate how our change makers engage with change and develop.

During the bi-annual friendly catch-up between Claudine and Simone, the program director for professional development at the business school Claudine sometimes teaches, they reflect on the latest news in the learning space. Claudine talks about what is happening in the start-up space and they exchange new ideas. Simone updates Claudine about the new ILP program that she is working on with a number of senior executives and learning experts.

She shares some new tools and methodologies for collaboration that are being put together. Claudine is very interested. It sounds like there is a way to bring together organizational and decision-making tools, with strategic approaches and latest methods involving the Sustainable Development Goals. Finally, something truly holistic. Claudine brings up the GAPFRAME, a tool that translates the Sustainable Development Goals into national priorities. She shares how she has been using it as a conversation starter with her clients. She shares how a food company has used it as their compass for setting strategic priorities. The idea of adding in co-creation and participative learning methods with strategic sustainability thinking and ways to improve an organizational governance sounds so exciting. She wants to know more about the business school's own experience with self-organization and wonders if there isn't a colleague who could bring some insight from that perspective. Simone smiles, she was thinking the same. They discuss options to introduce the topic and how

to test it. They consider possible fee structures for the program and discuss also how Claudine can scale the program and be remunerated for her efforts.

Christoph, the business executive, who we have met in the first chapter, is engaged in many important activities outside his company. He adds value where he can. This afternoon he receives a phone call from Simone who thanks him for his contribution to the new impact leadership program they have been working on together. She enthusiastically shares how his insights have helped finalize the program overview. The program will provide companies with clarity on how social issues can generate both revenue and income. Music in Christoph's ears. They walk through the latest ideas of how the program will teach managers how to work outside of the boundaries of the organization and more easily with stakeholders with different priorities.

Christoph works in a taskforce at his company to identify new strategies based on the Sustainable Development Goals. They had three sessions so far and started to see how difficult a challenge it is. Simone updates him on the GAPFRAME and explains how the tool can be used as a conversation starter to prioritize burning societal, environmental, economic, and governance issues against one scale. Christoph is relieved, that is exactly what he needed. He finds it so difficult to prioritize among all the many issues and the megatrends. Which one is more important and what should a company best focus on? Simone explains that the strategy tool to be used in the program is designed for companies to translate these priority issues into clear business opportunities.

As Christoph hangs up the phone, he looks at his paper. He has scribbled something vaguely resembling a heart with wings and feet. He shakes his head and smiles. He is very hopeful that this program will enable him to connect to both a larger purpose he feels inside and gain clarity of how to bring long-term value to his organization. He is keen to close the gap he sometimes feels between his deeper values and how his son misunderstands him. He sees a chance to deepen this alignment with this project and the attempt to connect the business strategy to what matters in society. Business sense makes personal sense.

The three change makers Claudine, Simone, and Christoph show how many different ways there are to contribute to change. Further below, we will meet another three change makers. For the moment, let us concentrate on the situation of Christoph's organization. Such a situation can apply to any organization of any size and in any sector.

Company leaders struggle to find answers for the emerging challenges of a fast-changing world

Organizations are challenged to position themselves in this volatile, uncertain, complex, and ambiguous – short VUCA – world. This demands an ability to step outside the prevalent thinking of a current strategy. It requires an understanding of the dynamics beyond the industry the business is currently in and a judgment of what megatrends may have an impact on the industry and competing industries and what this might mean for business. Beyond such defensive considerations, a progressive organization has the opportunity to consider how it might position itself in the context of new opportunities related to emerging challenges either on the environment or the societal front. The Paris Climate Agreement is such an example. What are the direct and indirect opportunities for your organization and how could the core competencies in your organization – those things of which employees are most proud – be applied to participate in new market activities? Answering these questions requires a combination of subject expertise and process knowledge.

A few weeks later, Christoph approached Simone with the idea of using his current strategic business problem as an action case for her Impact Leadership Program. His management team wanted to know business would develop into the digital age and what competencies the business would need to develop in order to keep its competitive edge in this fast-changing world. Christoph wanted to add a spin to ensure that they would also take the changing role of business in the context of the Sustainable Development Goals into account. Combining the two was personally essential to him and he was curious what Simone thought about this. Simone was delighted and confirmed his idea clarifying the potential for the company in the context of the program. She put him in touch with Claudine, the trainer and facilitator.

Claudine and Christoph fixed a skype call and they quickly connected. She asked a lot of questions about the issue he wanted to address. She was challenged to broaden her systems understanding and bring in her ability to provide a helicopter view since she was not very familiar with his topic. Christoph realized after a conversation with Claudine how easy it was for him to express his passion for business and the desire for his business to make a difference in society. He loved the sense of connection and opportunity he felt when Claudine helped him clarify the business proposition.

In a conference call, Christoph and Claudine brought Simone up to speed, who walked them through a short process of clarifying the

issue and defining the timeframe in relation to the Impact Leadership Program. Christoph proceeded to sign off the idea with his executive team and got the buy-in from his colleagues. He was starting to get really excited about this project. For Claudine, this was a most welcome way of applying her facilitation skill in a societal change process and she was really looking forward to facilitating this journey. In a next step, Simone invited Christoph to define the issue in further detail so that they could define the ideal stakeholder perspectives needed for the process. Christoph was not really used to working with non-business contacts or NGOs and was happy to have Claudine's support in reaching out to them. He realized there was some room for him to develop competencies on how to work with such broader stakeholders.

Lack of clarity about the issue results in lack of clarity of the process and the roles of those involved

Experience has shown that the preparation before such a stakeholder event is as critical as the event itself. Such an initial phase as well as the need for careful planning along the entire process is often underestimated. There is a tendency to get started and a focus on immediate results that are visible. While such energy and drive help overcome a sense of helplessness often associated with starting a complex process, it is the key risk of project failure early on. When looking at the success and failures of the early phase, we have identified a number of problems that occur when there is a lack of preparation for what is to come. Problems include a lack of clarity of the issue and a lack of clarity of the role and the purpose of the initiator. Also, there are conflicting expectations among those who eventually take part in a Collaboratory. In addition, there is missing clarity regarding the outcome expectations of such a process. How do we know when we are done with the process? There may be mixed messages that the initiator uses when issuing invitations to various stakeholders that can trigger confusing interests and perspectives when these stakeholders eventually show up for the Collaboratory. We have noticed that there is insufficient stakeholder mapping to appreciate different perspectives in a room. As a result, there is no transparency on the motivation or the underlying motives of Collaboratory participants. Finally, yet importantly, there are competing views on how to best run the underlying process of co-creation along the various phases of solving a societal problem.

Diversity among participants is key for co-creation and a source of disagreement and creativity

The effectiveness of a co-creative multi-stakeholder process lies in the diversity of participants. Some are change makers, others not. That is fine. Not every participant needs to be a change maker. What is important is to find people with a relevance to the topic at hand, people who care about the issue, who have something at stake. Well, stakeholders!

What we have shown here is an example of two projects meeting and the result is a creation of a better overall initiative. There is a program manager with an appetite to run a new program aimed at developing responsible leaders in the context of the 21st century. She had reached out to business leaders in order to create a needs-based and current-issues program. She also needs businesses to contribute real cases so that the students can work on real business projects. The project that Christoph has is perfect for this program. He wants his company to innovate in the area of the Sustainable Development Goals (SDGs) but has limited resources and time to set it up all himself and quite happily has the overall organization and process run professionally by an external facilitator in the context of a business school.

Such combinations are frequent and somewhat unpredictable. They relate to what Christoph, the network entrepreneur, is concerned about. How to know when a combined project is more appropriate than doing something alone. When is collaboration effective, when a distraction? There are no easy answers to this and finding clarity in the jungle of emerging initiatives, in the field of social transformation, is becoming increasingly complex and challenging. The example provided in this chapter serves to illustrate this point of collaboration and invites you to consider solutions beyond the typical process steps that are suggested in the next chapter. These serve as building stones for a process only. There may never be a process that looks exactly like what we shall describe in great detail.

Light that fire and have that conversation of achieving positive impact with a change maker near you!

More importantly, change makers live everywhere and can be found in many likely and unlikely situations and positions. You may know more change makers than you realized. Maybe including yourself. By providing further examples and short stories of likely and unlikely change makers, you may recognize elements of a change maker in yourself or somebody you know, love, or work with. If so, have a conversation with that person, you included!, and see if you can light the fire of change!

Eleanor is in her late 40s. She teaches economics at a business school. She has two kids in the late teens. She wonders to what degree her struggles at home with her kids are similar to those that she experiences in the classroom every day. Sometimes she walks out of class and she wonders whether her students have any attention span left at all. They seem to be unable to concentrate for more than five minutes. Recently, she has this creeping suspicion that somehow she's losing control of the classroom. Her models are being questioned, and she feels challenged in her expertise that she has built for so long. The questioning of students has not left her cold. She has started wondering whether her models still hold up to the scrutiny of nowadays reality. At the same time, she wonders why she would worry. After all, she graduated with a PhD from a top university. But today's economic realities no longer reflect many of the core economic ideas she has learned to love and appreciate.

A few months ago, Eleanor was invited to moderate a facilitated space with students in a new transversal program her school. They called it the GapFrameWeek. She was really struggling with her role. She had taken it for granted that her value lies in being an expert in her field. Yet here in this GapFrameWeek, she was required to "hold a space for students to learn," and to define their own questions so that they could develop creative solutions around economic issues. She felt nervous and uncomfortable, and she didn't know how to deal with such a new role. Simone had told her to be comfortable with uncertainty, to embrace the space of not knowing, to dare to keep the silence. But this freaked her more out than anything else. For what would she get paid, after all, if she didn't have to be an expert anymore? Surely, more is expected of a teacher than just to be a facilitator. What are all these methods of reflection, of silence, that remind her somehow of meditation and all those spiritual practices, that she finds very much out of place in a university setting?

These struggles at the business school remind Eleanor of an evening discussion she recently had with her oldest daughter. She is refusing to start a Bachelor degree after high school, something both her parents insist is best for her. The oldest daughter wants to go out in the world. She wants to make a difference. Immediately. She doesn't want to waste her time learning outdated concepts of business or economics. If anything, she would love to study sociology, or maybe literature. Psychology sounds interesting as well. Or maybe languages. Eleanor's husband Peter has suggested that maybe she study international relations, but she just rolls her eyes. "I don't want to become a diplomat." While Eleanor understands her daughter in some ways, she's also very much concerned

for her. What will happen if she doesn't get a university degree? How will she secure an income, and make her life in this world? As far as she can see, a university degree is the minimum requirement to have any guarantee for an interesting job later on in life. But this world is changing and that sure doesn't help!

Jannick is in his 30s and trying to set up his own consulting company. Having held a number of jobs in the corporate world and in a couple of NGOs, he is focused on finding a way to bring in his passion for making this world a better place. He has two young kids, and his wife also works. Their shared duties at home mean that he can spend time with his two young boys while securing ways to make ends meet. Jannick has an eternal hunger for learning and for understanding how he can become a more effective change agent.

He is challenged by the cost involved in continuous education, and he wonders if he will be recognized for all the courses and workshops where he learned all those invaluable tools to create effective change. If it were up to him, he would invest every other weekend in a workshop with other passionate change makers. His trouble is how to ensure he is paid for doing work that he loves, work that is aligned with his passion and values. He has done so much on a voluntary basis, and he keeps contributing for free to two projects he really cares about. Yet he's struggling to find a reliable and dependable source of income. Secretly, he is wondering whether all the workshops are paying off and if he can translate the acquired competencies into a recognized market value.

During the weekly couples' debrief, he brings up his worry about the lack of measurable impact. His wife reminds him of how hard he is working, and he wonders why then he can't shape more change. What is wrong? He has worked hard on aligning his inner values with the work he is passionate about, and yet there is a gap. His passion doesn't yet translate into the reliable income that he needs and deserves.

Marianne sits on the board of an innovative business school and is particularly excited about hearing what this school has been up to in the past year. The innovation ideas of the business school often inspire her with new insights she can bring back to her own business schools, where she has been Dean for the last four years. She has had an accomplished career as a professor and has published a number of important concepts and studies that have positioned her well among her colleagues. She takes great pride in the relationships and friendships that she has been able to build across the various institutions of higher education over the past decades. She is very dedicated to making a difference at the institutional level now for her school, even though she is in a way puzzled with recent developments in higher learning. To what degree,

for example, rankings require her school to focus in ways that make it harder to compete and to differentiate, with too many other schools trying to publish in the same topic journals as her professors are. Marianne is listening today to the board meeting, with the hope that she learns of more innovative and creative ways to teaching and learning. She is fully aware of the challenge of how difficult it is to bring that back to her faculty that has its eyes on the significant pressure to write articles and conduct relevant research, and to contribute with their institutional service with very little time to ponder deeply about how to be more effective in their teaching.

In recent meetings with her students, she couldn't but notice to what degree the courses that are taught at other business schools are no longer what students are hoping and wanting to hear. Students are asking for more applied and more up-to-date courses. They notice a gap between what they're being taught and the changing global realities, including the changing economic realities. She is puzzled with how much silence these demands are met by her colleagues in the faculty. She knows it's not the silence of resistance. She knows it's a silence of not quite knowing what to do. Silence of being uncomfortable. Her job as a dean is to translate what they have, which is a brilliant vision, in a way that differentiates the school from all the others. But that vision requires them to develop students as change agents for this world, and if students claim that this is not what they are getting, then she must change something.

Max is in his late 30s. He lives the dream of the new generation. He and his partner live in a community that has transformed an old villa into different apartments. They meet every Friday evening for food and drinks in the super-cool community space they've set up. It has quickly become an insider meet-up for the creatives of the city. The community space has grown into a bar and a coffee place on weekends. Recently, he and his partner talked again about having kids, or maybe rather adopting kids. They are both conscious of the lack of perspective there is for the future generation, and they want to do what they can to make a difference for them while also having a fulfilled life themselves.

Max co-leads an important initiative that brings together projects and organizations that work on solving a burning issue in his country. He spends much time ensuring that existing initiatives and emerging initiatives meet and collaborate. This part of his job consumes more time than he likes. Every week a new initiative pops up, a new brand gets created, people get together in a new constellation to focus on something new. He struggles to understand where his biggest impact is. Should he continue to try and bring all these initiatives together and

ensure that they can be scaled rather than canceling each other out? Or should he just let go and focus on his own initiative? The organizational boundaries are blurry. While he wants his initiative to succeed, he knows its success depends on how he manages to collaborate with other related projects. He needs to build the visibility for his brand and his co-owners remind him how important it is to demonstrate the impact of their work to secure continuous funding.

On Friday nights at their community bar, he drinks a beer with a couple of his pals. He shakes his head in quiet disbelief. The spirit of competition is driving many of the conversations, even if the word cooperation is frequently used. Does nobody understand the difference? He struggles to figure out how to consolidate the need to protect the brand he has built in a collaborative way, and to ensure that the brand protection doesn't hurt relevance and impact. Sometimes these seem to be in contradiction. Max feels he's spending too much time trying to associate what he does with what others do and he wonders why this has become so central to his job.

A great process can channel the potential of emerging contributors into a small group of change makers!

The next chapter illustrates how different change makers contribute to solving the emerging issues of this world as defined by the Sustainable Development Goals (SDGs). As we have seen, there are very different types of people, with different dreams and ambitions, and holding different roles in various kinds of organizations. Simone, for example, is quite unaware of her implicit role as a connector and bridge builder. We haven't learned much about her personally and she exemplifies those among us who unconsciously do great work in the transformative field of social change. Claudine is a freelance trainer in her early 50s, happily divorced and totally energized by the endless new emerging consulting and training ideas to help bring about change. Her challenge is to translate her love for learning into valuable business propositions. Christoph holds an executive position in an international organization and now in his early 50s is struggling how to align his values with the priorities of his business. Eleanor is a teacher at a business school in her mid-50s, challenged to adapt her teaching style to the demands of a changing world. Jannick is an idealist at heart in his mid-30s with a burning desire to make a difference in this world. Marianne is an innovative dean in a business school who is wondering how to go about transforming business education so that future-capable leaders emerge, and business will contribute to solving societal issues. Max has his dream job

in a purpose-driven institution and is able to balance time between his dream of a future family and his professional activity. His only regret is that he spends too much time trying to align interests of too many new emerging organizations into a coherent overall structure, which somehow is escaping him more and more. By following the journeys of these change makers, we will be able to understand how we can measure progress across the process steps.

Summary

- There are different types of change makers. Many of them may not even be conscious about their role.
- There are different types of people, with different dreams and ambitions, and holding different roles in various kinds of organizations.
- Stakeholder engagement projects often come up as a surprise and are often the happy surprise of a good conversation. They are time-consuming to organize and require a lot of upfront clarity so that relevant people will show up with the right intentions to collaborate.
- No change process looks like another. Creating them is an art, not a science.

Reflection questions

- Do you recognize yourself in any of these change makers? Why, and why not?
- How could your energy and desire for change be fueled? What insights do you take from these stories for aligning your own life purpose with your work?
- Do you recognize anybody in your surrounding in these stories? How do you think the person(s) you recognize might benefit from you telling them that they either are change makers or have the potential to become change makers?
- Is there any concrete action you feel inspired to do as a result of reading this chapter? If so, what is it?
- Go and implement that action and once done, congratulate yourself for having taken a courageous step in actualizing your own change maker potential!

Further reading and references

Hillman, Os (2011): *Change agent: Engaging your passion to be the one who makes a difference.* Charisma House, Lake Mary.

Price-Mitchell, Marilyn (2015): *Tomorrow's change makers: Reclaiming the power of citizenship for a new generation.* Eagle Harbor Publishing, Bainbridge Island.

Thompson, Laurie Ann (2014): *Be a changemaker: How to start something that matters.* Simon Pulse/Beyond Words, Hillsboro.

Individual level:

Please take a moment to reflect on your personal strengths and experiences that can serve you in this domain of change.

Breath

Please take a moment to reflect on your personal strengths and experiences that can serve you in this domain of change.

Superpower #4 – the building blocks of co-creation

Clarifying expectations of all participants, again and again, is a key for successful collaboration

In the business school where **Eleanor** teaches, she has a group of engaged students who are eager, yet they seem to want to learn other things than she has to offer. They challenge her to be more open, and she is trying. She wouldn't necessarily admit it, but she feels overwhelmed and a bit scared. At a recent school event, she met Simone, who had shared with her the ambition of the Impact Leadership Program, which includes learning to apply facilitation skills. As Eleanor walked home, she wonders if such a program wouldn't be able to help her gain confidence in her effort of reinterpreting her role from an expert to what Simone has called a "learning designer." Simone explained the change she is experiencing in the classroom in a way she could finally grasp. She had always felt close to business, and she was curious about finding out how business was dealing with the challenges of today. She was in need of a positive experience in teaching. She liked the idea of working with a business practitioner and felt an opening to something new. A window to a new type of knowledge beyond what she had learned at university. Maybe, she thought to herself, this was a way for her to be recognized in this transformative space as a new kind of an expert.

As **Jannick** leaves his favorite co-working space, he feels a spring in his steps. He feels elevated and full of hope. On social media a friend had shared a post of Simone and contacted her. Simone has talked to him about the Impact Leadership Program where he can gain continuous education credits and learn about how to help businesses to transform themselves. Simone had shared with him the number of tools that will be used and that will enable him to translate his passion into the vocation. He loves the idea of being part of a space where he can

practice his co-creation skills and put them together with new strategy tools. He feels excited about the idea of working with like-minded people from different networks and industries and further expand his network. He realizes how hungry he is to be part of a learning community, and why Simone's program touches him. She had talked to him about a way to finance his learning and his appetite for learning as a way to gain the formal recognition he needs. He is considering crowdfunding as a tool and is curious to see how the technology can help him advance. Jannick is eager to go home and share with his wife what he has learned.

At the car-sharing drop off Max runs into Simone. She picks up the conversation they had a few months ago over a glass of wine, and how this inspired her to integrate his perspective into the Impact Leadership Program she has launched. Max wants to know more about the GAPFRAME that he has been following on social media. He wants to make sure that the program uses it. Simone explains that they use it as conversation starters. She updates him on the latest ideas of bringing together stakeholders. She shares the program design with participants of different backgrounds working together to positive impact, working as learning and consulting with organizations who want to embed the SDGs into their strategy. They talk about how this can also serve as a way to redefine how business, civil society initiatives like his own, and startups in the social entrepreneurship field can work together. Max realizes that it is about finding a new language that allows these different players to talk to each other. He sees opportunities to strengthen his own business model as a collaborative partner across sectors and industries contributing to resolve burning issues in his country. He sees an opportunity to raise additional funds from business, if he can demonstrate the competencies his organization and network have built over the years. He walks away thinking that the program offers a space for a continuous reflection about his role as a network entrepreneur and how he can better align the purpose of his organization with new activities to maximize the positive impact for a better world.

Christoph reaches out to Marianne, the dean of the business school where Simone is working. Together they look at space and location requirements for the first stakeholder meeting, and if it is better to meet at the company offices or in a neutral space. Marianne kindly offers the meeting rooms of the business school. She enjoys engaging with Christoph in the local language in which she was not so fluent. She loves working with other cultures and looks forward to this new experiment. Claudine, who joined them in the call, has a few ideas of how this program could be made even more effective, and she is delighted to hear that Simone is open for her ideas and that the program continues

to develop. She loves it. Christoph is ready to initiate a call for participation to the stakeholders that he has mapped, and Simone has secured the needed diversity of participants in the Impact Leadership Program. Christoph feels really excited about the year ahead of him and is curious about the ultimate outcome of such a new co-creative process with all these unfamiliar players. Claudine is very much at ease with this collaborative and co-creative spirit and suggests that they meet separately to better prepare him for the first event.

Starting the process well is so important. Understanding where different participants come from is a part of that. Each person brings a different background, different expectations, strengths and weaknesses, fears and hopes. Our change makers illustrate some of these. Obviously, there are also other kinds of participants in a stakeholder process, with very different kinds of expectations. The preceding stories are by no means comprehensive.

Clarity about expectations most critically applies to the person who becomes the initiator of a co-creation process. In the example we use, it is Christoph who will be most challenged in the early part of the process to bring clarity about a range of things. Christoph is the business executive who has launched this project as a part of the Impact Leadership Program. The facilitator, in our case Claudine, needs to have these answers to prepare the initial event that brings key stakeholders together. The questions that need to be clarified before the launch of a typically Collaboratory process include:

- What is the issue and how is it defined?
- What are the stakeholders that need to participate and how are they mapped? What perspectives are covered, and who are these individuals that represent these perspectives?
- How do we invite these stakeholders? What is the so-called call? What do we invite them for?
- What is the authority of the person who invites?
- What are the expectations of this collaborative adventure that we're undertaking, and how do we know when we will be done?
- Who funds this adventure and who energizes it?
- Over what period of time? How much time are we giving this project to succeed?
- Who will hold the space? Who will be the facilitator who will ensure that appropriate processes are introduced and embraced in order to advance toward a co-creative solution?

Not each of the questions relate to every co-creative process and that is part of the clarity as well. Different stakeholders often hold different implicit expectations and it is important to make as many of them explicit as possible.

A facilitator allows the initiator to focus on the ideas and the people, rather than the process

Bringing in clarifications about the process, about expectations, about roles is an important and ongoing task of successful multi-stakeholder collaboration. Process and project interruptions, or worse breakdown often find their origin in misunderstanding about one of these. Another issue that comes up is the question if the initiator can also be the facilitator. Often, this happens without anybody ever thinking about it. It is just the way to roll forward. I have been guilty of this and I have often witnessed this in processes in which I have participated. This puts the initiator into a double challenge. First, she really cares about the project and wants it to succeed. She has something at stake and an opinion about at least one of the perspectives of the issue and how they might have to be addressed. Second, she will be also pushing the project forward with all that she has, mostly without the ability to step back and only focus on the process and what might be needed as a next productive step. Wearing two hats is complicated for the person herself, and it creates confusion among those who participate. For example, a participant may wonder if his suggestion gets ignored because it doesn't fit the process or because it didn't match the prevailing opinion about the issue. Without clarity about when the initiator wears what hat, this double hat becomes tricky and may result in unexplained exits from the process.

Let's look at the value that a facilitator can add to an initiator and the process. A facilitator will help the initiator in the initial phase of the process to gain clarity about the issue and its perspective. Something that is difficult to be done just within one head. As we will see, a facilitator also helps the initiator to round off the project in the end and to reflect on achievements. A facilitator is also very useful during the co-creative events, be they real or virtual. The role of a facilitator is to focus entirely on the process, not the content, allowing the initiator to be present in the content-related discussions and to engage fully where appropriate. The facilitator will be able to step back and assess what exercise and next step best serves the project and where the stakeholders are at a given moment, without any involvement in the content. If for any reason there is no facilitator available or the initiator wants to facilitate, it is important that the initiator steps back from contributing to the content, unless he specifies that the next statements come from him wearing the initiator's hat. Even for experienced facilitators, this is not a simple task; for a passionate initiator with limited facilitation skills, it is a very high ask.

Multi-stakeholder collaborations don't have the luxury of a traditional leader, as there is no formal hierarchy or power structure. It is supposed to

be a meeting of equals. Without that leadership function, it can get confusing who is in charge of what and who makes what decisions. Clarity about ownership and process help in such situations that are unusual for most participants who come from hierarchical structures or have grown up in them before. When an initiator facilitates, he needs to ensure that his opinion doesn't have more weight than the opinions of others. That is easier said than done and even unintended influencing can be manipulative in others' eyes. Hopefully, these points clarify the value of a facilitator and the risks of an initiator attempting to go through the journey without one.

There are two innovations in co-creation: a small cycle of rapid prototyping and a larger overall process

When designing a co-creative multi-stakeholder process, it is important to differentiate between the two different innovation cycles (see Figure 7.1):

• The small innovation cycle
• The large innovation cycle

The **small innovation cycle** builds around two connected multi-stakeholder events. The overall objective is to identify and develop solid prototypes

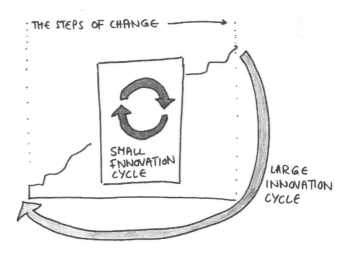

Figure 7.1 Comparing the small and long innovation cycles

solving the issue defined up-front. During a first Collaboratory, ideas are generated through a collaborative innovation process among stakeholders. This is followed by a prototyping phase that builds on the ideas generated with the objective to develop initial prototypes. This phase includes possibly additional new people than were present at the first or second Collaboratory. Once a small handful of prototype ideas are validated, a second Collaboratory takes place. An extended stakeholder group goes through a similar collaborative innovation process with the objective to substantially improve the initial prototypes. This is followed by a same prototyping phase where the improved prototypes are further adapted and improved with potential users and other solution providers. This small innovation cycle can take three to six months depending on how long it takes to gather the stakeholders for the Collaboratory and the speed and intensity of the prototyping.

It may well be that no satisfactory prototypes emerge after such a short innovation cycle. This will trigger a second small innovation cycle to start, clarifying again the issue at hand in order to invite relevant stakeholders for the Collaboratory event and the subsequent prototyping phase to advance the initial ideas into concrete business cases. The Collaboratory event can be virtual or real. The prototyping is always a mixture of both, as it depends on the type of idea that gets prototyped and where potential markets and suppliers would be. The short innovation cycle is completed once at least one, ideally three prototypes have advanced to a point where a realistic pilot solution can be implemented. A pilot solution is a product or service that can be marketed now, and is accompanied with a first business plan outlining revenues, costs, investments, and key success factors and partnership as well as distribution channels.

The **large innovation cycle** covers the entire co-creation process and includes the small innovation cycle. It covers nine separate building blocks that together constitute a success multi-stakeholder innovation process. In addition to the short innovation cycle, there are two building blocks at the beginning that the initiator needs to complete. The first involves gaining clarity about the issue to be resolved and the second addresses the need to understand the various elements and perspectives of the issue. The next two building blocks involve an initial Collaboratory event and an outreach and engagement phase. The first Collaboratory is all about creating the engagement and commitment of relevant stakeholders. It is about listening and hearing all the different perspectives from the participating stakeholders and agreeing on overall objectives and timelines. In the outreach and engagement phase that follows, committed stakeholders help identify further relevant partners that can be of help in finding prototype solutions. The initial question is clarified and sharpened. Upon completion of these four building blocks, we are ready for the small innovation cycle outlined previously and consisting of two building blocks, a Collaboratory and a prototyping phase that repeated at least once.

After the successful completion of the small innovation cycle, three more building blocks complete the large innovation cycle. One last Collaboratory event reflects on the prototyping journey and clarifies implementation steps. It is also the moment to celebrate and appreciate all the work done. The next building block consists of an outreach and engagement phase that aims to secure resources and partners for the implementation and sharing learnings of the process. The objective is to reach out beyond the stakeholders involved to share learnings and enable others to use and comment on the identified solution. The issue on which the team worked may relate to other issues that are out there. Recognizing that issues and solutions are often interrelated with other parallel projects can lead to new and bigger initiatives. And it may be that these are valuable next incubators for the solution identified.

An important last building block, that is frequently omitted, is all about the initiator closing the loop. The project is now closed. From an original idea, to a prototype all the way to a full-fledged pilot product or service along with a business plan, the initiator has led a co-creation process to fruition. There are numerous choices now. The initiator may choose to hand over the pilot to an interested third party, and to stop working on the project at this stage. Or she may stay engaged and adapt her life to create space to keep on working on this solution in a next constellation, in a new organization, initiative, or start-up. It is the moment for the initiator to decide if she wants to disengage from the project or to redefine her role forward. A future role will depend on what happens with the pilot. It may be transitioned into a separate organization, a project of an existing organization, or become a new collaborative multi-stakeholder initiative. The initiator had at the start committed to stick to the project for a certain period of time, without committing a lifelong engagement to it. This is an important decision point for the initiator that the facilitator can help make more consciously. This is also when the facilitator steps out. It is equally important to have clarity about what it means to stop facilitation here in case the project is transitioned elsewhere. This completes the larger innovation circle.

It may happen that an initiator looks again at the issue and says: "I am glad we have done this, now it is time to look at something else." This reflection may be the start of a new large innovation circle, with the initiator wanting to work on a new issue, thus starting the co-creation process again. We call these serial social change initiators!

The co-creation sessions are the heart of process and the moment where magic is orchestrated

Let's see what such a first Collaboratory event might look like. We are using the "Ideate" day of the SDGX innovation process introduced in the previous chapter. It is a good way to illustrate the third building block in the co-creation process mentioned earlier.

Christoph, head of sustainability of the Swiss operations of a global multinational, is both excited and a bit anxious as he takes a last look at the odd set-up of the business innovation day, for which he has invited a dozen experts from different departments and regions. It was not easy to convince them to dedicate a day to this "outside-in" exercise and he is happy to rely on two experienced external facilitators to guide them through the day. As his peers gather around the coffee bar, he introduces the day as a unique opportunity for everybody to think outside of the box and to envision the future of the company based on the societal and environmental challenges out there. He apologizes for the absence of his boss who had a last minute priority meeting at the company headquarters abroad.

The group is well prepared and ready to go. Each of the participants has completed a True Business Sustainability self-assessment of their company, has come to understand the value of an "outside-in" perspective that should enable them to translate the Sustainable Development Goals (or SDGs) into long-term business opportunities. The facilitators share the results of the online surveys and compare priorities that participants identify as important with those of the market they are in: Switzerland. The GAPFRAME provides a snapshot overview of the burning issues in Switzerland and serves as a conversation starter for the day. The morning is spent in various constellations around one key question: how do core competencies of the company match with burning issues in Switzerland. Beyond the products and services that are currently on the market, what is the company truly good at and how might these competencies be used in entirely new ways to offer services together with other players to solve three of the SDG issues that Switzerland is most lacking in.

The afternoon is spent in world cafés, brainstorming, fishbowl, and moment of open space to now innovate initial ideas around the three identified issues. In ever evolving constellations, the diversity of the team kicks in and new ideas are born, drawn up, pitched, revised, improved, dropped, renewed, and re-presented. The fishbowl serves to listen with new ears. First the senior team, the old-timers, discuss among themselves the implementation challenges these new ideas might face in the current organizations. Then the newcomers, having quietly listened to the old-timers, challenge their thinking with fresh innocence that occasionally has a touch of genius. The day ends with a round of pair-sessions to develop some initial broad-stroked action plans for the top ideas to be further developed in the prototyping phase. The group is enthusiastic at the check-out: nobody thought such creativity was possible in a single day.

It is time now to take a systematic look at the nine building blocks of a co-creation process. Figure 7.2 provides an overview including a view of the small and large innovation processes.

We differentiate between three types of activities:

A.   Clarifications for the initiator
B.   Events with the purpose of co-creating solutions
C.   Phases of scaling, outreach, and engagement

Each of these contain three specific activities that, when put in the right order, comprise the foundation of a successful co-creation process for multi-stakeholders. Not every block is needed in every process. This is a schematic support to change makers so that they can master-design their own process.

The facilitator will be mostly interested in the three events and might be requested by the initiator to help along the clarification blocks. The scaling and engagement blocks are really for the initiator and stakeholders to do, here the facilitator has no direct value to add as his role is not to be the project manager.

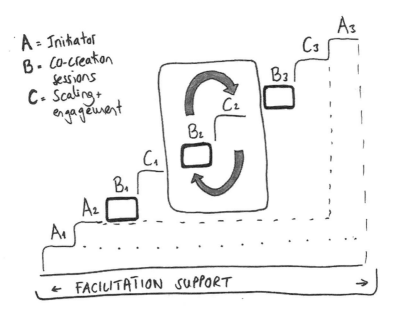

Figure 7.2 Overview of the nine building blocks of the co-creation process

The nine different building blocks of a co-creation process cover the initiator, co-creation events, and scaling

Let us look at each building block separately, in order of how they are most likely to be used:

A1: the initiator – finding an issue

The whole process gets started when a person, whom we call the initiator, picks an issue to be resolved through a multi-stakeholder co-creative process. The initiator needs to understand the personal relevance and the stake that exist with regard to the issue. It is important to clarify the desire and willingness to create a space for solving the issue. The initiator needs to understand and define the timeframe of the commitment and engagement that is required and necessary to make available for this whole process.

A2: the initiator – identifying perspectives of the issue

The initiator now defines the issue in more detail and with more granularity, including potentially a geographic focus. The stakeholders need to be identified and mapped so that they understand who might be participating versus who might be missing, and what the individual perspectives might be. It is important to secure the required resources for the length of the process, which includes also the facilitation support. The initiator launches a powerful call for participation to identify the stakeholders.

B1: co-creating event – building on the perspectives

This kickoff event serves to set the expectations, the overall timeline, and the process for the event. It is important to create an atmosphere and a setting whereby all present stakeholders can express their individual perspectives with regard to the problem so that the issue is understood in all of its dimensions. Together, all the present stakeholders will envision an ideal future where the issue is resolved. From this ideal vision, a first future-inspired series of prototypes is emerging. Through self-selection, it will become clear which stakeholder has more energy and interest in each of these co-created initial prototypes.

C1: scaling and engagement – securing engagement

It is important to secure the voluntary commitment of the initial group of stakeholders that were present in the B1 event and to invite them to a next event to follow-up on the prototypes. It is also important to secure the required

resources, which may involve also fundraising, for the process that is about to take place. This can include location cost and more. Relevant players need to be identified who can contribute to prototype solutions that were identified in B1. Relevant players need also to be invited to a next co-creative event. It is time to develop a rough initial communication strategy for this issue and the process. At the minimum, this includes a hashtag, possibly more.

Now starts a small innovation cycle that consists of B2 and C2, and will repeat with another B2 and C2, and possibly another round of B2 events and C2 engagement processes, depending on how things go.

B2: co-creating event – prototyping pilot solutions

This is about integrating additional stakeholders in the co-creation process without starting from scratch again. It is important that they are welcomed, heard, and feel included in the process. The initial prototypes are advanced into viable solutions, which also includes rejecting prototypes through a fast-fail process. It is time to start to develop business models for those prototypes that look viable. The event ends by selecting a few (2–3) small pilot projects.

C2: scaling and engagement – testing pilot solutions

To get started, the required funding needs to be secured and partners identified for the pilot phase of the selected pilot projects. Once completed, it is time to start conducting a reality testing of the small pilot project or projects. For this, the engagement of key players for a future implementation of the pilot project is crucial. Once tested, it is necessary to integrate the feedback of stakeholders and users that has resulted from the reality testing and from discussions of engaging future players.

In the small innovation cycle, we will be going back to B2 to do another round of solution creation, and another round of reality testing (C2), until we end up with a satisfactory pilot that we feel has a realistic chance of implementation.

B3: co-creative event – reflecting on the journey

This is all about identifying success factors to secure the implementation of the pilot by collecting ideas and support to transition to the next phase and enable, hopefully, a successful implementation. Time is spent to recognize the various contributions, the innovations, breakthroughs that we have achieved, and all other elements that are relevant for the success story that we are creating here in solving this issue. It is also important to reflect on learnings that have occurred through the inevitable failures, setbacks, disappointments, potential sabotage, and breakdowns so that we can share them with others for future learning as well.

C3: scaling and engagement – securing implementation and sharing learnings

The engagement desire of all participants for the future needs to be tested and clarified. The success story that was built is shared in all relevant networks. Others, who may not have been involved but to whom the solution of our issue is relevant, can thus become aware of what was achieved and assess to what degree they might want to participate in the implementation. It is time to find parents and godparents for the project, people and institutions/organizations interested to adopt and advance our pilot project. This is also about sharing lessons learned as a way to contribute to the change-maker community.

A3: the initiator – appreciating contributions and progress

It is important to clarify the future role of the initiator. It is important to identify how to either hand over the pilot project and end the commitment of the initiator, or to continue with the implementation. This involves working on new forms of possible organization or processes that may follow. The initiator and the facilitator reflect about the process overall, the three challenge dimensions of the individual, the group, and the shared issue level, as well as the outcome of the whole co-creation process. The initiator completes his engagement with a final communication to all past and possible future players that have been involved or may be interested in continuing with the pilot project that we have identified to solve the issue.

Understanding the key activities in each of the building blocks provides clarity in process design

Table 7.1 shows an overview of all steps. In terms of timing, it is important to understand how much time such a process takes. The first two blocks that relate to the initiator (A1 and A2) are likely to take about two to three months. The second two blocks related to getting started (B1 and C1) are estimated at about two months as well. The small innovation cycle, which consists of steps B2 and C2, will take about five to six months. The launching phase (B3 and C3), which defines the project continuation and rounds off the stakeholder engagement, takes about one or two months. Lastly, the closing down phase (A3) completed by the initiator may possibly take another month. In total, we are looking at a minimum one-year process when we consider all building blocks and a simple loop small innovation process. It is probably realistic to count one year and a half as things don't always go as planned. It is important for the initiator, at the beginning, to understand the extent, engagement, and length of this process so that the initiator is not taken by surprise about what is involved here. This timing is calculated from a process perspective and is estimated for a part-time project for an initiator.

Table 7.1 Overview of key activities in each of the nine process building blocks

The 9 building blocks of multi-stakeholder co-creation

Getting started	**A1: the initiator – finding an issue** 1. The initiator chooses an issue to be resolved 2. Understanding the personal relevance & stake initiator has with the issue 3. Clarity on the willingness to create a space for solving the issue 4. Defining the commitment timeframe for the process **A2: the initiator – identifying perspectives of the issue** 1. Defining the issue in detail 2. Identification & mapping of stakeholders perspectives 3. Secure resources for the process & facilitation 4. A call for participation to the stakeholders
Gaining momentum	**B1: co-creating event – building on the perspectives** 1. Clarifying expectations, timeline, and process 2. Creating a space for listening to all perspectives 3. Together envisioning an ideal future with the issue resolved 4. Creating first prototypes from the ideal vision **C1: scaling & engagement – securing support for the issue** 1. Securing the continued commitment of existing stakeholders 2. Securing the required resources 3. Identifying and inviting additional stakeholders 4. Developing a communication strategy
Small innovation cycle	**B2: co-creating event – prototyping pilot solutions** 1. Integrating new stakeholders in the process 2. Advancing the prototypes into viable solutions 3. Developing business models for pilots 4. Selecting pilot project(s) **C2: scaling & engagement – testing pilot solutions** 1. Securing funding and partners 2. Conducting a reality test of the pilot 3. Engaging key players for the implementation 4. Integrating feedback from the tests and discussions
Scaling out	**B3: co-creative event – reflecting on the prototyping journey** 1. Identifying success factors 2. Ideas and support to transition to implementation 3. Recognizing contributions, innovations, breakthroughs of the success story 4. Reflecting on learnings from failures, setbacks, and disappointments **C3: scaling & engagement – securing implementation and sharing learnings** 1. Clarity on the future engagement of stakeholders 2. Sharing the success story with relevant networks 3. Seeking godparents to adopt the pilot project 4. Sharing lesson learned in the change-maker community
Rounding off	**A3: the initiator – appreciating contributions and progress made** 1. Clarity the future role of the initiator 2. Clarity on future form of project 3. Initiator's reflection about the process, the learning dimensions, and the outcome 4. A final communication to all involved

Summary

- A successful multi-stakeholder process consists of a number of building blocks. These cover three specific activities: those of the initiator of the project, those related to the co-creation event, and those related to scaling and engagement activities. Each of these can be divided into three building blocks for a total of nine.
- The facilitator is mostly involved in the co-creation events and may help the initiator in the activities specific to his role.
- There is a small innovation cycle consisting of a repetition of co-creation events and prototyping. Combining all nine building blocks is defined as the large innovation cycle.
- The nine building blocks can be grouped into five phases: getting started, gaining momentum, the small innovation cycle, scaling out, and rounding off. With exception of the last phase, each phase consists of two building blocks.
- A typical co-creation event consists of a multitude of stakeholder engagement and interaction exercises and workshops designed to balance listening, sharing, visioning, brainstorming, ideation, and early prototyping.

Reflection questions

- What are your insights as you read about the issues and concerns of various change makers? What surprises you, what resonates with you, what do you recognize in others?
- How has the previous part of the book helped you look at these challenges of change makers with new eyes? What is new in your observation?
- Pick a co-creation process with which you are familiar and assess which of the different phases or building blocks were used and what worked well.
- Consider the same process and consider which building blocks might have been omitted and how this has affected the result, the initiator, or stakeholder engagement.

Further reading and references

Dyllick, Thomas, & Muff, Katrin (2014): Students leading collaboratories. In: *The Collaboratory – a co-creative stakeholder engagement process for solving complex issues*. Muff, K. (ed.). Greenleaf Publishing, Sheffield, pp. 127–133.

Kahane, Adam (2010): *Power and Love – a theory and practice of social change*. Berret-Koehler Publishing, San Francisco.

Muff, Katrin (2014): Designing a Collaboratory: A narrative roadmap. In: *The Collaboratory – a co-creative stakeholder engagement process for solving complex issues*. Muff, K. (ed.). Greenleaf Publishing, Sheffield, pp. 229–245.

Schamer, Otto (2016): *Theory U: Leading from the future as it emerges*. Second edition. Berret-Koehler Publishing, San Francisco.

Watkins, Alan, & Wilber, Ken (2015): *Wicked and wise – how to solve the world's toughest problems*. Urban Publishing, Croydon.

Group level:

Please take a moment to reflect on your personal strengths and experiences that can serve you in this domain of change.

Senses

Please take a moment to reflect on your personal strengths and experiences that can serve you in this domain of change.

Measuring progress in co-creation

Each participant and change maker is challenged to develop new competencies when working co-creatively

The first four-day session of the Impact Leadership Program consisted of a one-day Collaboratory session whereby stakeholders openly shared their different perspectives on how Christoph's company could embrace the Sustainable Development Goals, which created an environment where everybody felt that they had a chance to talk and were truly listened to. In the afternoon, Jannick provided a particularly colorful vision of what the future might look like for the company, and Christoph was amazed by how creative and imaginative others could be. It was not the first time for Jannick to apply a Theory U practice and he reveled in this environment where he felt he could make a real difference. He realized once more the power of visionary thinking and how much he identified with a better future to which he wanted to contribute.

Eleanor, who had decided at the last minute to join and hoped to bring in her economics perspective of the issue, had a really tough first day. She knew she wanted to upgrade her competencies as part of her professional development, but she felt very much out of her comfort zone. For her, the visionary exercise of imagining a different future was just too much. She couldn't stop her thoughts racing which was really distracting during the exercise. In talking with Jannick, she realized that she had a lot of preconceived notions about alternative approaches in the check-out session; she impressed the rest of the participants with her vulnerability when she shared her struggles she had during the day. The way Claudine had facilitated this closing session made Eleanor feel good about having shared her struggles. She realized that being authentic was a new strength that nobody else had ever noticed about her and

with which she really connected. Being real was what has always been dear to her.

In the six weeks following this first four-day workshop, participants were invited to reach out to stakeholders to secure their commitment to a co-creation workshop and future contribution. Jannick connected Christoph to Max. While Max had not participated in the program, he was instrumental in helping Christoph deal with the ambiguity of encouraging relevant stakeholders to voluntarily engage in this initiative. Christoph had never had to pitch a project like this and he felt awkward having to reach out to people and ask them to volunteer.

Jannick and Max came up with an idea of how to use Max's social network to playfully reach out to additional stakeholders, so that Christoph would have the right people in the room in the upcoming co-creation session scheduled in the Impact Leadership Program. Christoph was appreciative of this extraordinary support and complimented Jannick for his innovative idea. Jannick hadn't realized how innovative he was; he had always thought that analytical thinking was his strength. He didn't realize how strong his social media competencies had grown.

In the second session of the Impact Leadership Program, the enlarged stakeholder group met for one day to build on the ideas of the initial session and to start developing prototypes. Max brought a part of his team to help innovate this part of the process. He had a real keen interest in working with Christoph's company, and he brought in some start-up social entrepreneurs who had worked on initial ideas that proved really helpful in the prototyping process.

It became evident that it would make sense to hold the follow-on session at the impact hub location across town. This is the place where all the social entrepreneurs were working and where the facilitation space had a more dynamic feel than the business school. Marianne, who was sitting in on part of the session, was more than happy to adapt the plans and to cancel the lunch and dinner of the next day to enable such a change. When Christoph thanked her for her flexibility, she smiled to herself. She was not used to be complimented for being adaptive to change. Typically, she was accused as being very stubborn and insisting on sticking to plans, and she was wondering to what degree this program had a positive impact on her too, despite the fact that she only participated in part of the sessions.

In the next six weeks until the third Impact Leadership workshop, Max and Christoph worked together at involving more social entrepreneurs also from other cities. Working with Jannick, Christoph started to realize that he had begun to listen differently than before and that he had possibly more to learn than to teach in this process. He was

clearly the senior of the two, and yet Max had a more relevant experience in how to work with social entrepreneurs and listening was really a skill that was worth developing more than he had realized. For Max it was quite a challenge to be as straightforward as required. He had a clear business interest in this project and was struggling with how open he could be about his interests and to what degree he needed to be simply helpful. After a long working day, Max and Christoph sat together over an early dinner and had a really good conversation about this. Christoph congratulated Max for his courage and his authenticity about bringing up such a sensitive issue. Both felt that they had grown a lot in this process, having worked so closely together in engaging others to participate in the prototype piloting.

In the third Impact Leadership Program workshop, the prototyping and testing were reviewed. Participants further improved the quality of the pilots into first business models and a long-term strategy for Christoph's business. Three weeks later, they presented these new long-term business opportunities to the colleagues in Christoph's executive team business. The reaction of his colleagues when hearing such out-of-the-box ideas was really uplifting to Christoph. He felt great confidence that he could bring value to his organization when aligning to his personal values and looking at the bigger picture. His executive team received the long-term strategic options very well and had a lot of questions that the team took onboard to consider in more detail and include in the final company presentation at the end of the Impact Leadership Program.

Superpower elements show similarities with process competencies but can't (yet) serve to measure progress

The preceding story elements show how much is going on in parallel during a collaborative process. In Part II, we have considered the development challenges at the individual level, at the group level, and for the facilitator holding the space to solve the shared issue. As outlined in Part II, pairing traits into polar opposites adds a certain dynamic to the reflection, while considering also how these can turn into negative traits when overdone and imagining an integration of opposite traits as a healthier and more realistic approach to go about changing one's responsible leadership profile. In this chapter, we are returning to a more simplistic one-dimensional perspective that considers key competencies and related traits along the learning journey for individuals.

We adopt this simpler lens so that we can measure progress along the way by tapping into individual learning states. We have found that using the Competencies Assessment of Responsible Leadership a useful and convenient tool for such a purpose.

The significant multi-level challenges of co-creation processes on the individual, the group, and the shared issue level have not yet allowed the development of a superpower measuring tool. Table 8.1 shows the significant degree of synergy and resonance between the superpower elements and the responsible leadership competencies; however, at this stage, I am not comfortable making any suggestions in a translation attempt. What I can offer here is a tool that provides insights into the status and the progress in core process competencies along the way. This tool is available both for the facilitator and individual participants as a way to reflect on the process-related dimensions of a learning journey.

There are several ways of measuring progress along a co-creation process. The learning and development dimension outlined here is a new and additional way of measuring progress beyond focusing on the issue at hand and the progress on developing solutions for it. Given the complexity of the process itself, we feel it is worthwhile enabling participants in such processes to self-assess their progress and to offer a facilitator a tool to assess hidden issues and potential barriers that may harm the process if not properly addressed.

Table 8.1 Synergies and similarities of the superpowers and Responsible Leadership Competencies

Superpower elements	Attribution of Responsible Leadership Competencies
Appreciation	Stakeholder relations, Change & innovation
Alliance	Stakeholder relations, Systems thinking
Support	Self-awareness, Stakeholder relations
Deep Search	Systems thinking, Change & innovation
Collaboration	Self-awareness, Change & innovation, Stakeholder relations
Mastery	Ethics & values, Self-awareness
Awareness	Self-awareness
Coherence	Change & innovation, Systems thinking
Resonance	Stakeholder relations, Ethics & values

Competencies of responsible leadership can serve as a frame for assessing the development of participants

Assessing the learning journey across the process can be achieved by identifying core competencies involved in the various process steps and enabling various stakeholders to self-assess themselves at any point in time. Imagine there was a way to assess the state of the entire stakeholder group throughout the process in order to gauge where potential blind spots may be that may prevent progress. Aligning the competencies required in each of the process steps with the Competencies Assessment of Responsible Leadership (CARL) does just that.

CARL defines responsible leadership in a broader way than traditional leadership and allows change agents in any role and in any type of situation to assess their efficacy in advancing change. Such situations include also so-called leaderless processes such as multi-stakeholder co-creation and other initiatives in the new space of diluted organizational boundaries.

CARL consists of 45 competencies across five responsibility dimensions and three action dimensions (knowing, doing, being). Table 8.2 provides an overview of the 45 competencies across the 15 competency fields. The resulting competencies grid provides an excellent basis for assessing the competencies of multi-stakeholder co-creation process participants, including the initiator and facilitator. The beauty of the tool is its convenient access and immediate results. Using latest behavioral economics survey technology, the response-time sensitive survey generates instant individual and group assessments for free (www.carl2030.org). The survey can be taken at any point during the process as a status review of anybody's individual or the entire group learning progress. An initiator and a facilitator may choose to take the assessment at the beginning and the end to have a basis to reflect on their learning development across the entire co-creative process.

How do these competencies come into play during the co-creation process? Comparing competencies of responsible leadership to the nine building blocks with their activities is a way to highlight specific competencies along each process step. In addition to responsible leadership competencies, there are other important competencies required to successfully accomplish the co-creation process. These competencies include project management, interpersonal competencies, teamwork skills, and issue-related subject expertise. While these are not measured in the CARL survey, they can be assessed through traditional existing project management assessments. The particular benefit of CARL is an assessment not only of competencies but also insights into the action dimensions in each competency dimension. The action dimension allows a more granular view on related knowledge, skills, and attitude needed in each phase.

Table 8.2 The 45 competencies of Responsible Leadership (CARL)

	Knowledge (knowing)	Skills (doing)	Attitude (being)
Stakeholder relations	• Methods to identify & integrate legitimate stakeholder groups • Seeing conflict as a foundation for creativity • Dealing with conflicting interests of stakeholders	• Initiating & moderating a dialogue • Respecting different interests to find a consensus • Developing long-term relationships	• Being empathic with a desire to help others • Being open & trustworthy • Appreciating the positive in diversity
Ethics & values	• Knowing what is right & wrong • Knowing your own values • Understanding dilemmas	• Critically questioning & adapting values • Acting according to ethics & own values • Being a role model	• Being honest & integer • Seeking fairness • Being responsible toward society & sustainability
Self-awareness	• Understanding the importance of reflection in the learning process • Knowing oneself • Understanding one's own strengths & weaknesses	• Learning from mistakes • Reflecting on one's behavior, mental models & emotions • Adapting the communication style	• Reflecting about oneself • Reflecting about one's own behavior • Sharing one's developmental challenges
Systems thinking	• Understanding how the systems works • Understanding interdependencies & interconnections of systems • Understanding sustainability challenges & opportunities	• Dealing with complexity & ambiguity • Estimating consequences of decisions on the system • Seeing the big picture & the connections rather than the parts	• Working across disciplines & boundaries • Defending a long-term perspective • Providing a trans-generational perspective
Change & innovation	• Understanding the significance of a motivating vision in change processes • Understanding the drivers & enablers of innovation & creativity • Understanding conditions, functioning & dynamics of change processes	• Developing creative ideas • Acting to bring about change & translating ideas into action • Questioning the status quo & identifying steps of change for a sustainable future	• Being open, curious, & courageous • Being flexible & adaptable for change • Being visionary in finding solutions for society's problems

Source: www.carl2030.org

Core competencies an initiator is challenged to develop in each of the building blocks of co-creation

While many of the responsible leadership competencies positively contribute in several of the building blocks, the following overview seeks to focus on the one core competency in each of the three action dimensions in each block and across the five phases for the initiator and regular participants. Given the particular challenges and requirements for the facilitator, the related competencies are explored at the end.

Getting started (concerning only the initiator)

Finding an issue (A1) requires competencies such as understanding interdependencies and interconnections of the system (knowledge), questioning the status quo and identifying steps of change for a sustainable future (skills), and the capacity of reflecting about one's self (attitude).

Identifying perspectives of the issue (A2) demands further competencies such as a good knowledge of methods to identify and integrate legitimate stakeholder groups. In terms of skills, it is essential to be capable of estimating consequences of decisions on the system, and a key attitude here to focus on is the ability to appreciate the positive in diversity. Table 8.3 shows an overview of the two building blocks and the related core co-creation competencies.

Table 8.3 Overview of co-creation competencies in the getting started phase

Getting started (for the initiator)	Competencies in process
	Knowledge (A) Skills (B) Attitude (C)
A1: the initiator – finding an issue 1. The initiator chooses an issue to be resolved 2. Understanding the personal relevance & stake initiator has with the issue 3. Clarity on the willingness to create a space for solving the issue 4. Defining the commitment timeframe for the process	A. Understanding interdependencies & interconnections of systems B. Questioning the status quo & identifying steps of change for a sustainable future C. Reflecting about oneself
A2: the initiator – identifying perspectives of the issue 1. Defining the issue in detail 2. Identification & mapping of stakeholders perspectives 3. Secure resources for the process & facilitation 4. A call for participation to the stakeholders	A. Methods to identify & integrate legitimate stakeholder groups B. Estimating consequences of decisions on the system C. Appreciating the positive in diversity

Rounding off (for the initiator only)

Appreciating contributions and progress is the last building block and concerns in particular the initiator. He will benefit from the following competencies to do well here: understanding one's own strength and weaknesses (knowledge), seeing the big picture and the connections rather than the parts (skills), and being flexible and adaptive for change (attitude). Table 8.4 shows an overview of the two building blocks and the related core co-creation competencies.

Core competencies any participants can further develop during a co-creation process

Gaining momentum (for the initiator and for participants)

Building on the perspectives (B1) and the related co-creation event requires the competency of understanding conditions, functioning, and dynamics of change processes (knowledge), the capacity to develop creative ideas (skills) and the ability to be visionary in finding solutions for society's problems (attitude).

Activities related to securing engagement for the issue (C1) demand particular co-creation competencies such as understanding the significance of a motivating vision in change processes (knowledge), adapting the communication style (skills), and working across disciplines and boundaries (attitudes). Table 8.5 shows an overview of the two building blocks and the related core co-creation competencies.

The small innovation cycle (for the initiator and for participants)

The co-creation event related to prototyping pilot solutions (B2) and its related activities requires a number of specific co-creation competencies

Table 8.4 Overview of co-creation competencies in the rounding off phase

Rounding off (for the initiator)	Competencies in process
	Knowledge (A) Skills (B) Attitude (C)
A3: the initiator – appreciating contributions & progress 1. Clarity the future role of the initiator 2. Clarity on future form of project 3. Initiator's reflection about the process, the learning dimensions, & the outcome 4. A final communication to all involved	A. Understanding one's own strengths & weaknesses B. Seeing the big picture & the connections rather than the parts C. Being flexible & adaptable for change

Table 8.5 Overview of co-creation competencies in the gaining momentum phase

Building momentum (for the initiator & participants)	Competencies in process
	Knowledge (A) Skills (B) Attitude (C)
B1: co-creating event – building on the perspectives 1. Clarifying expectations, timeline, & process 2. Creating a space for listening to all perspectives 3. Together envisioning an ideal future with the issue resolved 4. Creating first prototypes from the ideal vision	A. Understanding conditions, functioning & dynamics of change processes B. Developing creative ideas C. Being visionary in finding solutions for society's problems
C1: scaling & engagement – securing engagement 1. Securing the continued commitment of existing stakeholders 2. Securing the required resources 3. Identifying and inviting additional stakeholders 4. Developing a communication strategy	A. Understanding the significance of a motivating vision in change processes B. Adapting the communication style C. Working across disciplines & boundaries

including seeing conflict as a foundation for creativity (knowledge), acting to bring about change and translating ideas into action (skills), and being open, curious, and courageous (attitude).

The activities of test pilot solutions and thus to scale and securing engagement (C2) demand specific additional co-creation competencies such as dealing with conflicting interests of stakeholders (knowledge), respecting different interests to find a consensus (skills), and defending a long-term perspective (attitude). Table 8.6 shows an overview of the two building blocks and the related core co-creation competencies.

Scaling out (for the initiator and for participants)

Activities related to the co-creation event to reflect on the journey (B3) benefit from the following particular competencies: understanding the importance of reflection in the learning process (knowledge), developing long-term relationships (skills), and being open and trustworthy (attitude).

Securing a future implementation and sharing learning (C3) involves activities that can be significantly enhanced with the competencies such as understanding sustainability challenges and opportunities (knowledge), learning from mistakes (skills), and sharing one's developmental challenges (attitude). Table 8.7 shows an overview of the two building blocks and the related core co-creation competencies.

Table 8.6 Overview of co-creation competencies in the small innovation cycle

The small innovation cycle (for the initiator & participants)	Competencies in process
	Knowledge (A) Skills (B) Attitude (C)
B2: co-creating event – prototyping pilot solutions 1. Integrating new stakeholders in the process 2. Advancing the prototypes into viable solutions 3. Developing business models for pilots 4. Selecting pilot project(s)	A. Seeing conflict as a foundation for creativity B. Acting to bring about change & translating ideas into action C. Being open, curious, and courageous
C2: scaling & engagement – testing pilot solutions 1. Securing funding and partners 2. Conducting a reality test of the pilot 3. Engaging key players for the implementation 4. Integrating feedback from the tests and discussions	A. Dealing with conflicting interests of stakeholders B. Respecting different interests to find a consensus C. Defending a long-term perspective

Table 8.7 Overview of co-creation competencies in the scaling out phase

Scaling out (for the initiator & participants)	Competencies in process
	Knowledge (A) Skills (B) Attitude (C)
B3: co-creative event – reflecting on the journey 1. Identifying success factors 2. Ideas and support to transition to implementation 3. Recognizing contributions, innovations, breakthroughs of the success story 4. Reflecting on learnings from failures, setbacks, & disappointments	A. Understanding the importance of reflection in the learning process B. Developing long-term relationships C. Being open & trustworthy
C3: scaling & engagement – securing implementation & sharing learnings 1. Clarity on the future engagement of stakeholders 2. Sharing the success story with relevant networks 3. Seeking godparents to adopt the pilot project 4. Sharing lesson learned in the change-maker community	A. Understanding sustainability challenges and opportunities B. Learning from mistakes C. Sharing one's developmental challenges

Opportunities for competencies development for a facilitator along the co-creation process

Let us now also look at what the development opportunity is for the facilitator in a co-creative process. Unlike other processes, co-creation with multiple stakeholders represents a particular challenge in facilitation with its own set of competencies. Ideally, the facilitator plays an active role in six of the nine building blocks. These include on the one hand, the facilitation of all three types of co-creation events (B1, B2, and B3), as well as supporting the initiator (A1, A2, and A3). It is important to remember that the following competencies are not a comprehensive list of facilitator knowledge, skills, and attitude but concern only the specific additional competencies a facilitator is well served to have acquired when supporting a multi-stakeholder co-creation process. The facilitator is not necessarily involved in taking care and supporting the intermediary engagements and scaling processes (C1, C2, and C3) and therefore there are no identified competency developments noted for the facilitator in these three areas.

Supporting the initiator in finding the issue (A1) involves understanding how the system works (knowledge), being a role model (skills), and seeking fairness (attitude). The stance at this early stage sets the tone for the entire process and is therefore particularly important. Enabling the initiator to identify relevant perspectives (A2) consists of understanding the drivers and enablers of innovation and creativity (knowledge), dealing with complexity and ambiguity (skills), and being responsible toward society and sustainability (attitude). At the end, when the initiator is invited to appreciating contributions and progress (A3), the facilitator is well served with competencies that include knowing yourself (knowledge), reflecting on one's behavior, mental models and emotions (skills), and being honest and having integrity (attitude).

Facilitating co-creation events that seek to build on hearing the various issue-related perspectives (B1) is enhanced with competencies such as understanding dilemmas (knowledge), initiating and moderating a dialogue (skills), and providing a trans-generational perspective (attitude). Facilitating events focused on prototyping pilot solutions (B2) requires specific competencies including knowing what is right and wrong (knowledge), critically questioning and adapting values (skills), and being empathic with a desire to help others (attitude). Facilitating a co-creative event with the objective to reflect on the prototyping journey (B3) benefits from competencies such as knowing your own values (knowledge), acting according to ethics and own values (skills), and reflecting about one's own behavior (attitude). Table 8.8 shows an overview of the two building blocks and the related core co-creation competencies.

Table 8.8 Overview of co-creation competencies for the facilitator

The relevant building blocks for the facilitator	Competencies in process Knowledge (A) Skills (B) Attitude (C)
A1: the initiator – finding an issue 1. The initiator chooses an issue to be resolved 2. Understanding the personal relevance & stake initiator has with the issue 3. Clarity on the willingness to create a space for solving the issue 4. Defining the commitment timeframe for the process	A. Understanding how the systems works B. Being a role model C. Seeking fairness
A2: the initiator – identifying perspectives of the issue 1. Defining the issue in detail 2. Identification & mapping of stakeholders perspectives 3. Secure resources for the process & facilitation 4. A call for participation to the stakeholders	A. Understanding the drivers & enablers of innovation & creativity B. Dealing with complexity & ambiguity C. Being responsible toward society & sustainability
A3: the initiator – appreciating contributions & progress 1. Clarity the future role of the initiator 2. Clarity on future form of project 3. Initiator's reflection about the process, the learning dimensions, & the outcome 4. A final communication to all involved	A. Knowing oneself B. Reflecting on one's behavior, mental models & emotions C. Being honest & integer
B1: co-creating event – building on the perspectives 1. Clarifying expectations, timeline, & process 2. Creating a space for listening to all perspectives 3. Together envisioning an ideal future with the issue resolved 4. Creating first prototypes from the ideal vision	A. Understanding dilemmas B. Initiating & moderating a dialogue C. Providing a trans-generational perspective
B2: co-creating event – prototyping pilot solutions 1. Integrating new stakeholders in the process 2. Advancing the prototypes into viable solutions 3. Developing business models for pilots 4. Selecting pilot project(s)	A. Knowing what is right & wrong B. Critically questioning & adapting values C. Being empathic with a desire to help others
B3: co-creative event – reflecting on the journey 1. Identifying success factors 2. Ideas and support to transition to implementation 3. Recognizing contributions, innovations, breakthroughs of the success story 4. Reflecting on learnings from failures, setbacks, & disappointments	A. Knowing your own values B. Acting according to ethics & own values C. Reflecting about one's own behavior

The status and development of individual competencies is the biggest blind spot of social change projects

Often, multi-stakeholder processes are used in a learning context. These are isolated processes that happen often next to other professional activities of the different players, often in a rather auxiliary manner. When co-creation takes place in real life, there is a significant danger for ignoring the process and paying too much attention on the end result and output of the process. It is important to acknowledge that given the particular nature of multi-stakeholder co-creation, the end result is heavily affected by the developmental progress of all involved players. In our experience, this is mostly ignored and represents a serious blind spot in social change.

In the fourth and last session of the Impact Leadership Program, it was time to take stock of what had been achieved. Different elements of success were identified. Eleanor took a key role in summarizing key contributions from various stakeholders, particularly innovation steps and breakthroughs that together represented the core success elements of the process represented. She felt very comfortable, her analytical strength enabling her to look back and reflect over the one year process with ease. She had learned to take an appreciative perspective in this reflection and as a result felt more at ease with her report than she did in the past. She surprised herself with how natural this new habit already felt.

As facilitator, Claudine helped collecting lessons learned from failures, setbacks, and disappointments that participants had experienced over the past year. She enabled not only the collection of items, but created a space for a deeper reflection, using the ideas that these setbacks can be considered as sources for growth and learning. This was one of her key strengths. She had always loved such tricky moments in the facilitation process. She sensed how the group relaxed into this challenge despite the tensions that had occurred and were not always addressed at the right time. Having the possibility to reflect openly about both positive and negative experiences made the group want to celebrate and appreciate what they had accomplished together, on both an individual and a group level.

In round-off work, Jannick volunteered to reach out to other groups that worked together in solving societal issues. He offered to share the success stories and lessons learned with the groups to which he was connected. Christoph also looked together with Max for ways to connect their idea beyond the country that they had focused on to see if in other geographic regions anybody had an appetite to apply the idea or collaborate with them.

Marianne was in the room when the teams presented the final report to the companies and their executive teams. Her presence contributed in a very important way to the overall success of the process when the CEO of Christoph's company became a bit defensive and expressed feeling overwhelmed with the sheer scale of what was proposed. She found a way of breaking the strategy into smaller steps and to walk him and his team through ways to consider the work ahead in a lighter and more collaborate spirit. She suggested that involving others in the company would not only secure the chances of implementing the strategy but also serve to upgrade the competencies of other leaders. She shared her experience about how another company had connected the implementation to their HR competency development plan. At the end of the session, Claudine stepped up to Marianne and congratulated her for her ease in applying her team-working and collaborative strengths in a situation of high pressure.

At the end, Christoph and Claudine reviewed the entire process for Christoph and had an open conversation about his personal development, his contributions, and challenges in group processes. Christoph reflected that it had not always been easy for him to follow the unfamiliar innovative process, but the increasing trust in Claudine made it easier for him to let go and to "just go with the flow." As a gesture, Claudine brought Christoph a small clay sculpture that she had made – she was an artist on the side – and with the note that this was a symbol of his strength for his future journey. Christoph smiled at how unusual it was to receive a handcrafted gift in the digital age. He so appreciated her gesture.

Simone looked through the feedback forms of the 32 course participants, evaluating to what degree they had indeed advanced in the 18 core competencies that the Swiss-based executives had identified as most critical to develop in such a program. In addition to Christoph's project, six other companies had worked on their long-term strategic plans in parallel. As she read the comments, she felt deep gratitude for having been a part of such an innovative, deep-change program. There was solid progress in all identified competency dimensions and she reflected on how she could share this outcome with the 15 CEOs. She also looked at how the participations faired in their Responsible Leadership Competencies as measured before the course and after the course. She was impressed by the degree of change across the knowledge, skills, and attitudes dimensions and decided to propose this assessment as a standard to future editions of the program. Simone also received many ideas of how to further improve the program. She booked an innovation meeting with the concerned facilitators and experts to discuss these insights and already looked forward to next year's program.

Summary

- The stories of the change makers illustrate the number of parallel change and development processes that are happening during a multi-stakeholder process. These are both conscious and unconscious and impact positively or negatively the process and the outcome.
- Being able to assess and measure the learning and development status along the different phases of a co-creation process can be truly insightful and allows one to address possible blind spots that may be hindering the project process. Framing the development challenges in the context of responsible leadership competencies allows measuring a so-far ignored dimension of multi-stakeholder collaboration.
- The Competency Assessment for Responsible Leadership (CARL) offers an excellent basis to assess specific competencies along the co-creation process. The 45 competencies aspects are grouped into five competency dimensions: stakeholder relations, ethics and values, self-awareness, systems understanding, and innovation and change. They are also split into the three action dimensions of knowing, doing, and being (knowledge, skills, and attitude). These CARL competencies can be measured at any time along the process either by a single individual or the entire group. The short, free online assessment provides instant feedback including development recommendations.
- There are key competencies in the area of knowledge, skills, and attitude for each of the nine building blocks. Three of these competencies are related to the initiator, while the other six competencies relate to any type of participant. In addition, there are competencies that concern facilitation activities in six of the nine building blocks, supporting the initiator and facilitating co-creation events.
- The learning context of the Impact Leadership Program has inspired the translation of responsible leadership competencies along the process steps of stakeholder co-creation. There are also other leadership-related competencies that are worthwhile developing beyond those connected to multi-stakeholder processes. An effort with CEOs has resulted in identifying 18 critical competencies of future leaders and we have portrayed how seven change makers develop these as a part of the Impact Leadership Program. This example shows that there are several ways of looking at competencies.
- The 45 traits of responsible leadership are not recommended to be used to develop one's responsible leadership competencies. When developing competencies, it is useful to put single traits into a more dynamic setting of matching them into polarity pairs, considering also negative dimensions of the traits when they are over explored and to imagine an integration between traits to achieve a superpower of performance (see

Chapters 3, 4, and 5 related to how to achieve this at the individual, group, and shared issue levels).

Reflection questions

- Take the free online CARL survey on www.carl2030.org and read your individual assessment report. What strikes you in particular about the report?
- Look at competencies where you score well (3–4) and describe situations where you have used these strengths.
- Look at competency domains where you have higher development potential (1–2) and read the suggested further development recommendations. What insights do you gain when considering how you can further improve?
- What are the benefits of embedding a co-creation process in a learning framework such as the Impact Leadership Program? What are the drawbacks?
- As you look at the 18 future-relevant competencies developed by Swiss-based CEOs, what observations do you make? What strikes you as you compare these to the 45 competencies of responsible leadership?

Further reading and references

Competency Assessment for Responsible Leadership (CARL): https://carl2030.org/ accessed March 18, 2018.

Impact Leadership Program: www.katrinmuff.com

Muff, Katrin: *Leadership Competencies Survey*. Unpublished data accessible on request through katrin.muff@bsl-lausanne.ch

Muff, Katrin, Liechti Anna, & Dyllick, Thomas (2018): The Competency Assessment for Responsible Leadership (CARL) – consolidating the Responsible Leadership discourse into an online tool. *Journal of Business Ethics* (in review process). Article accessible via katrin. muff@gmail.com until publication

Smit, Arnold: About CARL. *Soundcloud*. https://soundcloud.com/business-school-lausanne/ interview-with-dr-arnold-smit-by-tony-johnston, or via https://carl2030.org, both accessed March 18, 2018.

Shared issue level:

Please take a moment to reflect on your personal strengths and experiences that can serve you in this domain of change.

Silence

Please take a moment to reflect on your personal strengths and experiences that can serve you in this domain of change.

Part IV

Co-creation for organizations

It is widely acknowledged that business is an important driver to bringing about the positive change we need to live well on this planet. The innovation power of business is unparalleled and can move mountains. In times where legislation is lagging behind the dynamics of change, soft law becomes a good indicator of upcoming risks and opportunities. The number of reporting initiatives on corporate responsibility in different industries is a lead indicator to anticipated future legislations. Companies can take a proactive or reactive stance in this. This book advocates a proactive attitude and invites organizations to voluntarily engage in the sizable opportunities that emerge from solving the sustainability issues related to the SDGs. Matching core competencies of a company with burning issues in a region can result in powerful new long-term business opportunities that will secure the company's economic future. This chapter is about a clear and simple process that starts with external issues and translates these into strategic opportunities and long-term business alternatives.

Intra-organizational change makers, or intrapreneurs, are a key success factor to initiate, drive, and sustain such challenging processes of change. Leaders who seek to acquire future-relevant skills are well served in stakeholder co-creation processes as these add a capacity to lead not only within organizational boundaries but also outside of it. Collaborating with other players in co-creating solutions is among the most desired competencies of future leaders as our research shows.

Chapter 9 combines existing tools and processes in an applied way for organizations to embrace stakeholder co-creation in a current strategic process that can enable internal change at the same time. Building on the SDGs, the SDGX innovation process serves to scale organizational transformation toward sustainable development. It offers a hands-on process for multi-stakeholder co-creation for organizations. Change makers can use this process or use elements of the building blocks to create their own co-creation process. Strategic processes have evolved in the past decades and a review highlights the challenges for an organization to become future-ready.

If Part IV could be summarized by one image, it would be Figure IV.1. Experience shows that companies and individual change makers are dramatically more effective if provided with pragmatic tools of co-creation. Chapter 9 will explore the GRIPS process offered by www.sdgx.org, as a solution to effectively implement

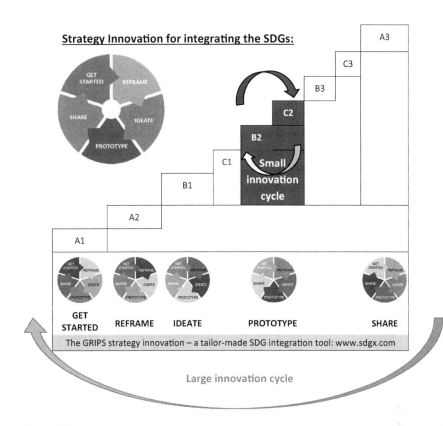

Figure IV.1 Overview of the co-creation process in a ready-made corporate tool SDGX.com

the large innovation cycle that is needed when an organization seeks to redefine its strategy. Even more so, this is needed in the era of the SDGs, where an orientation toward societal and environmental issues can be translated not just into new revenue streams but enable an organization to survive in these times of dramatic change. The small innovation cycle is called prototyping in the GRIPS process and has been tested with numerous organizations around to world to ensure high quality investment proposals for new business propositions. This image is important because it illustrates an underlying desire of this book: to enable individuals and organizations to figure out how to effectively co-create so that all of us can live well on this one great planet we call home. It is in this hope that the tools are proposed.

Superpower #5 – The positive-impact tool of organizations

For your tailor-made co-creation and change process, play with the building blocks

Jannick is at the coffee place ahead of time. He is eager to advance and is happy that Claudine was able to see him. He has done his homework and prepared a one-page overview defining his issue that he is keen to resolve. His youngest son is suffering from diabetes and he has become a ferment defender of healthy breakfast and lunch options for kids. He has also completed an initial map of concerned stakeholders he would like to have included. He wants to work with the food labs of Nestlé that is scaling their content-reduced sugar crystal innovation that maintains taste while reducing sugar intake significantly. He has a couple of food retail chains on the radar. He must be able to convince the regional authorities to participate so that they amend food regulations in primary school canteens and he wants to see how a start-up working on climate friendly food can contribute. He has prepared tailor-made pitches to each stakeholder group outlining the project idea and why this is relevant to them. He has a date and a location in mind. Now, he needs to convince Claudine to join him as his preferred facilitator. She needs to be remunerated and he still must find a project sponsor. He knows that getting support of a sponsor is a good reality test for the implementation chances of the project. He is nervous but hopeful. He has contacted the consumer representatives, the parent association, and a couple of international associations located in Switzerland. He may even do a kick-starter initiative. Finally, Claudine is showing up!

She has great news. At a network meeting, she talked to the owner of a healthy snacks start-up and mentioned Jannick's project to him. He is not only willing to join but also to finance two co-creation sessions and have a social media expert help with outreach. As they review the process building blocks that Jannick anticipates through the tight

seven months' time window until the summer break, they discuss how they can save time and short-cut some of the time-consuming outreach phases. It greatly helps that both of them are familiar with the Collaboratory building blocks and have experienced a multi-stakeholder process together. They advance fast and productively.

Claudine orders a second espresso and leans back. "Jannick," she says, "tell me, what do you see as your biggest personal development challenge in this process? What do you want me to help you with during the reflection process?" Jannick smiles. He is ready. He pulls out a further sheet and hands it ceremoniously over to her. They are ready to go!

The preceding story illustrates one way for a change maker to apply his future-readiness to advance a societal issue. It shows how a change maker selects an issue that is close to his heart and then starts to better understand the issue and mapping stakeholders to frame the different perspectives. These are the first two building blocks of a successful co-creation process, as outlined in Chapter 7. Following these building blocks systematically is one way to advance. There are other ways too.

A change maker may look at the issue at hand and then selectively pick among the building blocks as he deems appropriate. He may choose to engage in talks with related stakeholders before deciding to go ahead and decide how much time and energy to invest. He may choose to focus only on the small innovation cycle first and see if he can kick-start an innovation fast with limited effort.

If he is a change maker operating within an existing organizational structure, he will likely need to limit his time as initiator and find a process he can sell to his company. This is much like we have seen Christoph in the previous chapters. Or, a change agent may choose to join an innovative educational program that includes a co-creation project as part of its curriculum design, as we have seen in the example of the Impact Leadership Program. As an addition to the previous chapters, this chapter will focus on providing a pathway for intra-organizational change makers and we will outline practical steps for them here as follows.

Organizations need processes that work internally and connect with relevant players externally

Let us now look at how a co-creation process would look like when driven by an organization with an appetite to change its products, services, or market strategies and is looking for ways to access the untapped opportunities connected to the Sustainable Development Goals (SDGs). According to the 2017

Better Business Better World report, there are over 60 market opportunities that relate to country and business issues, with the potential to generate more than US$12 trillion in new revenue by 2030, and create over 380 million new jobs globally. Accessing these opportunities requires organizations to embrace and address complex issues and to work with players outside of their usual market place. This is where effective stakeholder co-creation tools come in. When looking for new business opportunities in new markets that develop from societal or environmental issues, the ability to work with stakeholders outside of the boundaries of your organization has become key for success.

Integrating such new opportunities into the existing business operations is a further challenge. Enabling change in an organization means connecting its strategies to the transformational journey of its people while aligning its mission to regional or global concerns the organization has a competency to help resolve. And yet, the ability for an organization or a network to change depends on its change readiness. This change readiness is an integral part of the organizational culture and can be assessed to select the most appropriate process. Successful change happens when the individual, organizational, and societal levels align and interact. This is where intra-organizational change makers, also called intrapreneurs, come into play!

When organizations drive co-creation processes with a tight set of practical tools and processes

This book has so far focused primarily on the process aspect of co-creation. In this section, we focus on a combination of tools and processes to answer to the call of business leaders for simple answers to the complex challenges of identifying long-term business opportunities derived from the SDGs. It is useful to take the SDGs as an example given the sheer number of new emerging tools at this moment. While this picture is a reflection of a certain moment in time, it may still be helpful to analyze tools that emerge after the publication date. I suggest segmenting them by their implied action dimension. This can mean a tool either provides knowledge, or enables action, or seeks to achieve a behavioral shift.

Figure 9.1 shows that there are tools that provide knowledge, others enable action, while yet others work on the transformational aspect of behavior. These action dimensions are also called knowing, doing, and being. In the knowing dimension, we can differentiate between tools that are conceptual frameworks, such as the SDG Compass, the SDGs, or True Business Sustainability, and tools that offer data or information for analysis, such as the SDG Index, the GAPFRAME, or the CEO guide. In the doing sphere, there are tools such as Future-Fit, the Earth Security Group (ESG), and Project Breakthrough. These can be considered as hands-on process tools for business. There are also transformative tools such as the SDGXCHANGE that is discussed further later. It is connected to data sources and conceptual frameworks from

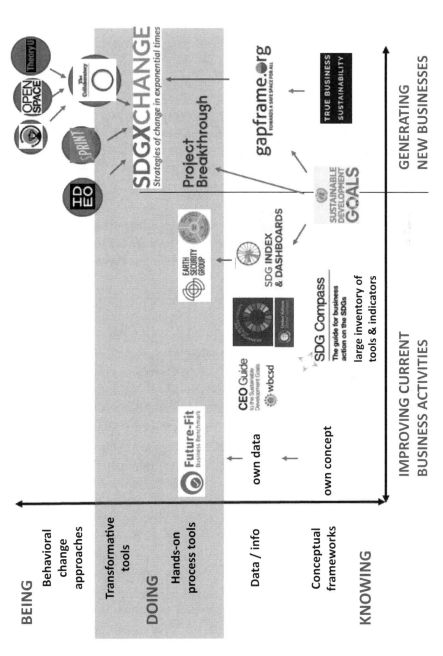

Figure 9.1 The action dimensions of tools in the SDG landscape (as per early 2018)

the knowing dimensions, and is enriched by a variety of process tools that fall into the being dimension. These tools include Theory U, Open Space, IDEA, the Collaboratory, SPRINT, CARL, and more. It is interesting to note that few content or knowledge tools are offering an integrated approach including also tools in the doing or being area. And yet, we know that change cannot be accomplished by knowledge alone.

There is an additional perspective covered in Figure 9.1 that is important to highlight here. There are a majority of tools that implicitly are oriented to help an organization in its continuous improvement. These are operating from what might be called the existing paradigm in which the role of business is not further investigated. Tools that focus on generating new business are explicitly those that take a more expansive view on the role of business, and see opportunities far beyond current markets and the current operating logic of a firm. Such tools seek to tease business beyond its current comfort zone and suggest to look in new services areas where they will deliver entirely new solutions that are derived from solving existing societal or environmental issues "out there," rather than figuring out what to do with existing resources "in here." This outside-in perspective is developed in the True Business Sustainability typology and suggests that the real purpose of business is far more than just business (see Figure 9.2).

Our experience in working with numerous organizations has showed that this perspective change from inside-out to outside-in is a mindset shift that is

Business Sustainability 3.0

Inside – Out

Outside – In

- Risks & opportunities for current business

- Reducing negative impacts ("the bads")

- New white-space opportunities

- Making positive contributions ("the good")

Figure 9.2 True Business Sustainability differentiates between an inside-out and an outside-in perspective (Dyllick/Muff, 2016)

essential before organizations are able to consider societal and environmental issues, or the SDGs, as true opportunities. Such a mindset shift needs an appropriate process and a space for a deep conversation.

Another important element, we have discovered, of such a conversation is to have clarity about what the burning issues are in a country or region in which an organization is active. The personal concern matters as much as pure facts. In talking with organizations' leaders, we learned to start the conversation from where leaders were at the time, wherever that was. For this, we had asked them to share with us what issues they personally cared most about, what issues they felt their organization should engage in, and what they thought was most important in their country. Gathering the different inputs to these questions provided a fertile ground for an excellent conversation that brought a deep engagement from all participants. To frame this discussion, we developed and now use the GAPFRAME, which translates the SDGs into national priorities, as shown Figure 9.3 for Switzerland. In this example, being able to compare diverse issues such as biodiversity, clean energy, equal opportunity, sustainable consumption, and social integration provides a rich context for lively discussions among participants. The GAPFRAME, beyond its scientific value, has emerged to add most value as a discussion opener among stakeholders to discuss how a single issue relates in the context of a country and how priorities compare against personal preferences or agendas.

The SDGXCHANGE strategy tool is a combination of tools and processes enabling organizations to embed the SDGs by embracing this extended business perspective and focusing on working on effective solutions in a co-creative approach with relevant stakeholders. The outside-in perspective and the Gapframe are included in the first three steps of the innovation process and serve to set the stage for prototyping ideas of a truly different nature than what an organization currently does.

The SDGX innovation process shows how the co-creation building blocks work with corporate strategy

In 2017, my colleague and business sustainability expert Barbara Dubach and I prototyped a methodology with four Swiss companies that fast-tracks such a co-creation process for organizations with the specific wish to integrate the Sustainable Development Goals (SDGs) into their corporate strategy. The outcome is a pragmatic strategy tool called SDGXCHANGE which includes an easy and convenient five-step process that applies the co-creation building blocks for a strategic change process in organizations. This SDGX innovation process is featured on the dedicated website: www.sdgx.org (see Figure 9.4).

We will illustrate the steps of this process for intra-organizational change makers. We do recommend the use of a trained facilitator, a SDGX Adviser (see website). Change makers can of course also design their own processes

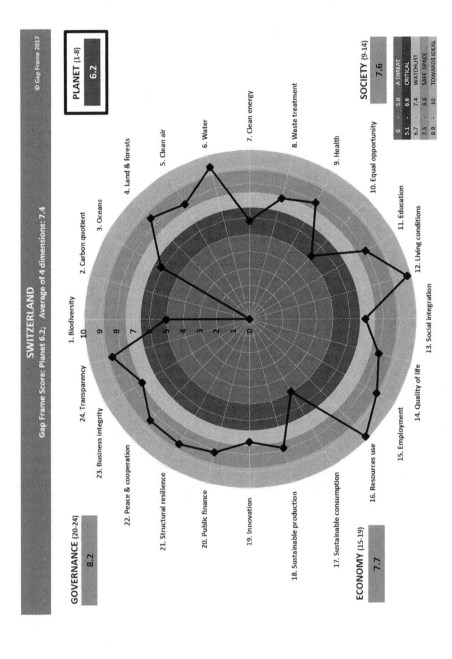

Figure 9.3 Burning issues for Switzerland – translating the SDGs into national priorities (www.gapframe.org)

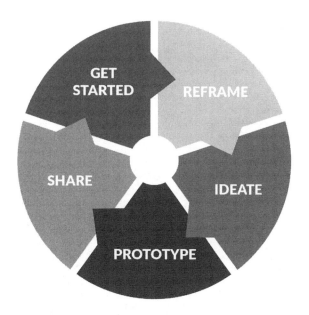

Figure 9.4 The SDGX innovation process translating SDGs into long-term business opportunities (www.sdgx.org)

and use different tools, and are not bound to use an external facilitator, but appoint their own. You can consider the SDGX innovation process as inspiration to create your own process.

The five steps of the SDGX innovation process are:

- **Get Started:** Assessing change readiness and the sustainability status of your organization
- **Reframe:** Clarifying the SDGs as business opportunities and shifting from inside-out to outside-in
- **Ideate:** Engaging key players in co-creating new business opportunities
- **Prototype:** Developing new solutions with new clients for net positive impact
- **Share:** Assessing prototypes for impact and sharing success stories.

They relate to the building blocks of co-creation as outlined in Chapter 7 as highlighted in Figure 9.5. As we can see the initial two GRIPS phases replace the initial two activities that a typical initiator would be engaged in when identifying an issue and learning more about it. When organizations drive change, they have a similar assimilation phase to accomplish, which the SDGX innovation process calls "Get Started" and "Reframe." At the end, the process step of the initiator (A3) is adapted for organizations, which at that

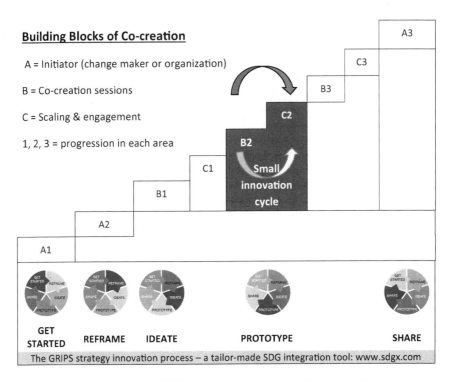

Figure 9.5 Comparing the SDGX innovation process with the building blocks of co-creation

time measure and share the outcome to the larger community, the "Share" step. The scaling and engagement steps are downplayed in the SDGX innovation process in order to gain speed and momentum in the context of organizational decision-making. This implies that these "C"-related steps will come in only once the company has made its investment decision after the completion of the Prototyping phase, which is a translation of the "Small Innovation Cycle" outlined in Chapter 7.

Let us understand in brief what each of the GRIPS steps entail.

GET STARTED is about identifying the starting place for an organization. For this, we are interested in learning more about an organization's change readiness. Establishing the cultural readiness, helps identifying the path of change for the company matching the rate of the change on a scale from small incremental change to true quantum leaping. Building on the Competing Values Framework developed by Cameron and Quinn and enriched with insights of Mitzlaff, we differentiate between four different types of cultures, each of which has a different change readiness profile. Acknowledging its culture profile, an organization can be facilitated through the change process accordingly. Understanding an organization's position in the Business

Sustainability Typology (BST) provides further food for thought at the beginning of a strategic change process. The two short online assessments were developed to evaluate different levels of change readiness and integration of sustainability in business. The outcome of the two surveys offers an excellent starting basis for the senior management and strategists to reflect on their current versus desired organizational culture relative to the change they anticipate. They also serve to develop a common language between the internal change maker and other key players in the organization.

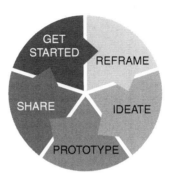

REFRAME is all about preparing the minds of key stakeholders for the shift in thinking that will be needed in the first co-creation event. For this, we have developed another online survey that all participants of the next phase will complete prior to the event.

For business to embrace Grand Challenges such as the SDGs as opportunities for long-term new markets, it is necessary to start looking at what these challenges are out there and which of these may relate to a participant and to the organization. Three questions are answered here: when looking at the GAPFRAME issues, a translation of the SDGs into national priorities, (1) what issues do I personally resonate most with, (2) which issues do I think the company can best address, and (3) looking at the priorities in the country, what should we be focusing on.

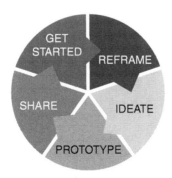

IDEATE is a multi-stakeholder co-creation day as we know it well from the nine building blocks. There it is coded as B1 and seeks to integrate perspectives in order to undertake a first visioning and open space workshop series dedicated to identifying early ideas that can be further developed into prototypes. Ideally, there are about 15 participants in the room (virtually or real) for the day. The morning is dedicated to reflecting on the results of the Get Started and Reframe phases. These reflections then lead to a co-creative matching of core competencies of the companies with the priority issues in the regions as identified in the GAPFRAME. Identifying what a company is truly best at, finding those competencies which stand out of which employees are most proud and that are unrelated to products and services produced, is a phenomenal and truly enriching process. Comparing these to the burning issues in society is where magic can happen. By lunchtime, the three most interesting issues are selected and serve as the basis for the innovation process in the afternoon. In a deep reflection space, the group splits in two and holds an interesting fishbowl inner-outer dialogue about implementation challenges that may occur when looking at the ideas identified in the afternoon. The outcome of the day is at least three early developed ideas with rough action plans for next steps and longer term goals.

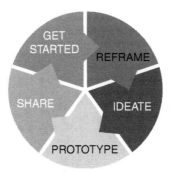

PROTOTYPE is the phase that is called the "small innovation cycle" in the nine building blocks in Chapter 7. For organizations, we have smoothed the approach in either an intense four-day sprint or a two to three months' long process with four innovation events that can be held virtually. The purpose here is to further develop the ideas from the last phase by testing them with potential clients and in new market constellations, including new partners and discarding or improving them to the point that the ideas become prototypes. Once solid enough for more serious testing, initial business plans are developed to estimate the additional revenue and the bottom-line impact in order to acquire support and resources for an implementation. Scaling across further regions is a next step here that then takes us into further months and compares to the later fourth phase of the nine building blocks.

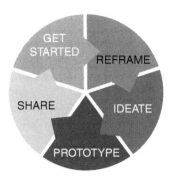

SHARE contains both elements of the fourth and fifth phases of the multi-stakeholder process as well as further steps not specifically addressed in the pure co-creation process. In particular, corporations are keen to summarize results and use them in their annual reporting. We also suggest that they contribute their best practice examples to a newly developed web initiative called the Business Sustainability Today, a platform consisting of videos of such best practice examples of advanced sustainability companies. The Focused Reporting initiative offers hands-on advice in how to go about to provide sustainability reporting that measures up to the completeness requirements as outlined by the WBCSD in their Reporting Matters approach, but also to the creditability and relevance criteria, building on the GAPFRAME and RepRisk reports.

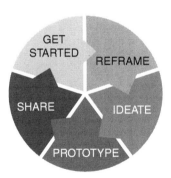

The entire process is compact and streamlined, allowing internal decision makers to quickly grasp initial resources requirements and estimate the impact of approving the launch of such a process an internal change agent would request. Figure 9.6 shows an overview of all process steps visually.

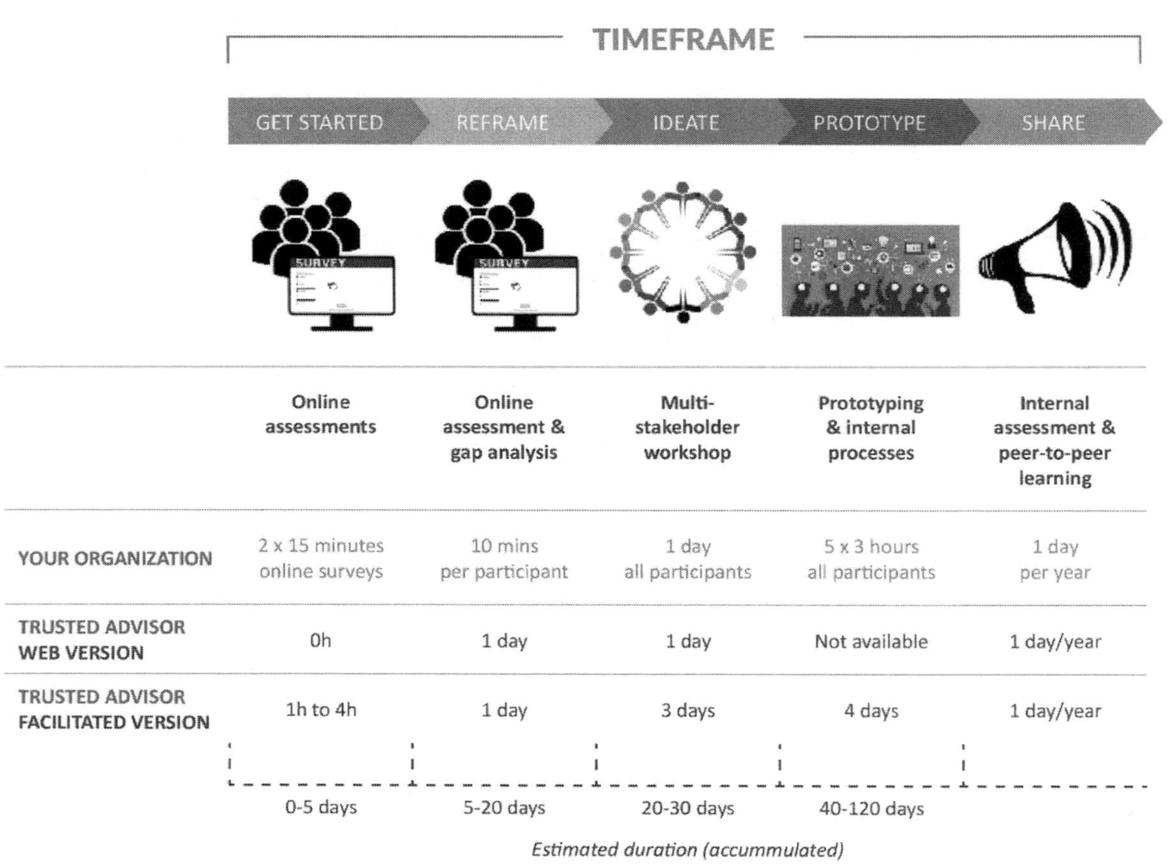

	GET STARTED	REFRAME	IDEATE	PROTOTYPE	SHARE
	Online assessments	Online assessment & gap analysis	Multi-stakeholder workshop	Prototyping & internal processes	Internal assessment & peer-to-peer learning
YOUR ORGANIZATION	2 x 15 minutes online surveys	10 mins per participant	1 day all participants	5 x 3 hours all participants	1 day per year
TRUSTED ADVISOR WEB VERSION	0h	1 day	1 day	Not available	1 day/year
TRUSTED ADVISOR FACILITATED VERSION	1h to 4h	1 day	3 days	4 days	1 day/year
	0-5 days	5-20 days	20-30 days	40-120 days	

Estimated duration (accummulated)

Figure 9.6 Overview of the steps of the SDGX innovation process (www.sdgx.org)

Solving pressing societal issues challenges the strategic thinking processes of organizations

There are increasing discussions about how organizations are governed and how their decision-making and strategy processes fare in a fast-changing world. Do these need to be changed to ensure that the company can become future-ready? Is there a need for adopting decision-making processes to enable a shift from a status quo position in terms of cultural readiness to a change maker status? In terms of strategy development, it has become obvious that shifting from a traditional top-down strategy development to an iterative bottom-up top-down approach is closing the gap with what is really going on in the field and with the people in the organization. People have earned a new position in strategy considerations; they are no longer blind implementers. It has become clear that a strategy must resonate and inspire them if a company wants to ensure a successful implementation. While inspiration may happen when a vision is announced from the top, resonance is the result of a personal connection and relevance, which only occurs through a direct involvement.

Organizational Development practitioners have long struggled with the question of how to achieve change in organizations. In the 1950–1960s, when organizations were considered as organisms that adapt to their environment, organizational change was understood as a "planned change" paradigm that consisted of three steps: create a vision, get buy-in, execute. Since the 1980s this approach has been questioned and further developed as a result of having to deal with "adaptive challenges" – problems that are so complex that no one knows the right answer upfront. In the past twenty years, organizations are seen as complex responsive processes of emergent "meaning making." Dialogic Organizational Development (DOD) suggests that organizations are "conversations." A place where people make meaning of their experiences through narratives and stories, with the prevailing ones creating and sustaining the socially constructed reality that defines an organization. DOD practitioners have built methods and tools around the idea that an organization is a place where any action results from self-organizing as a result of these prevailing conversations. DOD builds on the understanding that reality is socially constructed and consisting of multiple realities with the truth emerging step by step. DOD practitioners approach change by creating new conversations that disrupt habits and meanings, in order to increase diversity for the benefit of innovation, and as a result energize motivated people to prototype transformational change.

In my three decades of professional experience, I have had the privilege to experience firsthand all three such approaches. The top-down strategy worked very well in a U.S.-owned multinational that operated in a slow-changing commodity business. The M&A team I was a part of could simply go and buy companies that fit the top-down strategy and grow the business internationally. In my first decade of professional engagement, work was easy and things were clear.

The fast-moving consumer goods company I worked for as Strategic Director for Europe, faced the challenge of the U.S. corporate strategy not working internationally. The country directors across Europe each had their own reason why they couldn't implement the strategy and needed to have it adapted for their own circumstances. In my indirect leadership role, I would gather the European country directors in peer-sessions to gain clarity of the complex European market and to define a common strategy. In my second decade, work was complicated.

In my most recent decade of work, I witnessed how we have transformed the business school I work at into a self-organizing structure using Holacracy as an operating system. There is no single understanding of what we are anymore. Depending on to whom I talk, I get a different interpretation, a different story. My colleague who dislikes Holacracy lives a story of how lacking self-organization is in terms of a unified strategy and she finds evidence for this everywhere she looks. Another colleague who follows Holacracy closely has determined that self-organization is only for certain people and unless we all get it, forget it. My own interpretation of who we are depends on the day and to whom I talk. It is a tapestry of my own stories interwoven with those of my colleagues. My sense-making journey depends on the prevailing story flavor of the week, which influences my strategic outlook accordingly. Work has become liquid.

Embedding sustainability opportunities into your strategy will change your organization and its governance

It is not a question of belief or of being right but a question of what organizational setting we operate in and in which context the organizations operate. In times of increasing rate and scale of change, we will see how long each of these different models can prevail and what further developments will emerge. Evidently, depending on the strategy approach of a company and its culture, a different path is needed when wanting to translate external Grand Challenges such as the SDGs as business opportunities. Understanding where a company currently stands in these terms is thus important for a successful co-creation process. In an attempt to offer a solution to any organization, Quinn has come up with the interesting suggestion of intrapreneurial change makers first writing a long list of change ideas and then picking a few based on three rules including that the idea can be implemented without asking for permission.

In the interest of getting organizations future ready, how does such strategy development relate to embedding sustainability into the organization? Does it make sense to keep a separate sustainability strategy? And if so, what are the limitations of such a strategy? Whether or not a company is ready to embed sustainability into the core of its corporate strategy or rather sees it as an

important side activity is reflected in where the company is positioned in the Business Sustainability Typology (BST) that is part of the Get Started phase of the SDGX innovation process.

Even a business-as-usual (BAU) company with no sustainability strategy at all, can ask the question "how do I translate the SDGs into long-term business opportunities"? The implications of the answers will simply be different than for a company that is operating at a BST 2.0 sustainability level, having developed a triple-bottom line understanding for the different types of values created. For a BAU company, it would be recommended to keep the SDG-innovation process separate from its existing organization, inviting those employees with an affinity and interest in it and to create if needed even a separate entity for such a prototyping space. This is a bit like R&D departments have traditionally worked: as relatively isolated units that would only interact with the organization once an innovation was developed far enough along to start considering how it can be best integrated in the current product offer, replacing or extending parts of the existing product range.

For a BST 2.0 company with a Clan culture, it may be possible to open up more externally across the entire organization with representatives across various business units being involved in a co-creation process with a variety of external stakeholders. The prototyping approach also includes being very aware of the organizational reactions to the project and to fluently adapt when needed to preserve the project and maintain the potential of the company intact.

Make the best judgment call you can at the beginning and then stumble forward a step a time. Stop to reflect, correct the direction if needed, and take the next step. The organization will be shaped by different stories and the more the co-creation process involves a diversity of people across the organization, the quicker new stories spread. With this, the organization will start to see itself differently and change is on the way.

Dare to stumble into stillness, void of inner and outer chatter, and sense the resonance of co-creation

We have now completed the journey and have come full circle. In Part III, we have focused on highlighting the challenges of co-creation in order to help change makers to become future ready. In this part, we have focused on how to make an organization future ready, addressing both challenges and pragmatic solutions that intra-organizational change makers can use.

Honoring also the key role of the facilitator throughout this book and a co-creation process, I would like to share three insights I have gained in my work as a facilitator and participant in collaborative multi-stakeholder processes:

Three different notions of becoming when taking on a big challenge:

- A notion of becoming "big." It relates to the experience of feeling connected to my true potential, embracing a stance that really suits me and working on a project that is entirely aligned with my values and purpose. A growing inner sense of feeling the potential to achieve big things (inside-out movement).
- A notion of becoming "small." As a result of experiencing true heart connections with other participants or regarding the issue as it relates to nature or animals, a lived experience that I am just a small part of something so much bigger than myself. A growing outer sense of feeling a deeply humbling connection with everything that is (outside-in movement).
- A notion of stillness. A growing notion of experiencing the difference of inner and outer chatter as one type of energy in me and in the room and the magic of stillness within me and resonance with what is around me (the experience of the shared issue).

May these reflections guide and inspire your journey. Please share your experience, feedback, and ideas with us on www.collaboratory2030.org. We are building a community of change makers so that you have a place to go when you are stuck or would like to share a great breakthrough moment!

Summary

- Change makers have various options to launch multi-stakeholder co-creation processes.
  - Entrepreneurial change makers can use the proposed nine building blocks of co-creation, or they can adapt the building blocks to fit their specific project.
  - Intrapreneurial change makers can either use the SDGX innovation process modified for organizational co-creation processes, or develop their own process building on the nine building blocks and the SDGX innovation process.
- For organization that seeks to integrate the SDGs into its core strategy, it makes sense to adapt the nine-step process suggested for change-maker initiated multi-stakeholder co-creation process. While the small innovation cycle still forms the heart of the process, the other building blocks before and after can be radically reduced.
- The SDGX innovation process outlined on www.SDGX.org represents such a simplified process developed specifically for organizations seeking to translate the SDGs into business opportunities. The Get Started,

Reframe, Ideate, Prototype, and Share phases are designed to enable organizations to work with multi-stakeholder in a targeted co-creation process.

- Defining the cultural change readiness and the current state of the sustainability journey of an organization are two critical elements when starting a co-creation process around the SDGs. Key players will hence develop a common language to discuss how radical a change process is appropriate for the current state of the organization. Free online assessments of both these elements are available on www.SDGX.org under the Get Started phase.

- The governance and decision-making process of an organization influences the approach of how to implement sustainability (or the SDGs) into its strategy. We differentiate between mid-20th-century top-down hierarchies, turn of the century adaptive organizations, and the latest emerging self-organizing structures. Irrespective of the type of organizational structure, it is worth considering the perspective of Dialogic Organizational Development that suggests that organizations are socially constructed ongoing "conversations." This means paying attention to the prevailing stories told inside the organization and how they are used as a sense-making mechanism internally.

- A key insight from co-creative processes, intra-organizational or independent, related to the notion of how such a process can make you "big" discovering new potential inside and "small" in the context of the big issue at the same time, and how with increasing awareness, there is a notion of a stillness that sets apart inner and outer chatter and opens a space for entirely new solutions to emerge.

Reflection questions

- What have you learned or realized in terms of how an in-company process of stakeholder co-creation is different from a change maker initiative?
- Is there any difference between a change maker who acts as an entrepreneur (realizing his own ambition by creating a new project or initiative) and an intrapreneur (processing his idea in an organizational context)? If yes, what are these in your view?
- Why is it important to be aware of the starting point of an organization in terms of their culture and sustainability journey when considering embracing a strategic process to integrate the SDGs into a company strategy?
- What are your reflections at the end of this book? What have you learned? What are you inspired to do? What is still unclear?
- Where can you go to find more answers?

Further reading and references

Business Sustainability Today website: https://sustainability-today.com/ accessed March 21, 2018.

Cameron, Kim S., Quinn, Robert E., DeGraff, Jeff, & Thakor, and Jannick V. (2006): *Competing values leadership: Creating value in organizations*. Edward Elgar Publishing Limited, Cheltenham.

Dialogic Organizational Developmental: www.dialogicod.net accessed November 21, 2017.

Dyllick, Thomas, & Muff, Katrin (2016): What does sustainability for business really mean? And when is a business truly sustainable? In: *Sustainable business: A one planet approach*. Jeanrenaud, S., Gosling, J., & Jeanrenaud, J.P. (eds.). Wiley, Chichester, pp. 381–407.

Dyllick, Thomas, & Rost, Zoe (2017): Towards true product sustainability. *Journal of Cleaner Production* Vol 162, 346–360.

Focused Reporting: www.focusedreporting.ch/ accessed March 16, 2018.

GAPFRAME: www.gapframe.org

SDGXCHANGE and the SDGX innovation process: www.sdgx.org accessed March 16, 2018; Organizational Culture Assessment Instrument (OCAI) www.ocai-online.com/ accessed March 16, 2018.

RepRisk: www.reprisk.com/ accessed March 16, 2018.

World Business Council for Sustainable Business: Reporting matters: www.wbcsd.org/Projects/Reporting/Reporting-matters accessed March 16, 2018.

Individual level:

Please take a moment to reflect on your personal strengths and experiences that can serve you in this domain of change.

Empathy

Please take a moment to reflect on your personal strengths and experiences that can serve you in this domain of change.

Part V

Conclusion

Chapter 10

The Five Superpowers
for Co-creators

So here we are. You made it through the book or you jumped right to this conclusion section (which is what I typically do). Let me share my summative thoughts about this book and its pretense to introduce the idea of superpowers in co-creation.

I have just read a good dozen of reflection papers of graduates of a recent Collaboratory training we held in Vienna Austria. We exposed our "apprentices" to the nuances of running a multi-stakeholder session and they discovered a complexity and ambiguity that they had never anticipated or encountered. Their personal accounts of how they grew in these situations and what they learned from them are humbling. Their own perception of how much more they have to learn is frightening. I wonder if we had overexposed them, complicated their learning journey with too many levels of reflection. And yet, co-creative collaboration is not a neat process that plays around pre-set rules and much can only be learned through experience and post reflection.

In this book, I attempted to go a step further. Beyond the one-day event, taking a step back and considering the entire co-creation journey a single project may go through. A big task, but a very necessary one. We must embrace such challenging projects that demands working with unfamiliar other stakeholders, competitors, maybe even enemies. And we have to raise above all of this and dare to walk on the water as we bravely learn to envision an ideal future towards which we shall find ways to prototype new solutions, never-dared collaborations, unimaginable approaches again and again, until it works. Crazy! This space is clearly a reserved domain of heroes. And a hero you are; yes – no less! And don't smile on this – if you read this page in this book, you are a hero, I'll sign a paper certifying this if you write to me. You are here because you believe in the need to acquire the skills and competencies to work through the wicked mess of working with stakeholders and you have invested time to learn a bit more about it. You rock and I wish I knew you personally for I know you are a part of a growing tribe of people who prefer to see the possible despite the growing evidence of the impossible. In the face of urgency and challenge, you raise my hero!

Which of the five superpowers spoke most to you? Where do you sense you have a natural strength or affinity? Which is most foreign and weird to you and you prefer to put aside for a while? Pick your favorites one or two and see how you can develop them further, using some of the suggestions provided here. Let me summarize the five superpowers again here (See Figure 10.1):

- Superpower #1: genuine engagement
- Superpower #2: collective solutions
- Superpower #3: transformative spaces
- Superpower #4: co-creation building blocks
- Superpower #5: positive-impact strategy tool

Superpowers 1 to 3 are three different aspects of the process – different levels of collaboration that need to be mastered to at least some degree to ensure that the collaboration can work. They are about the HOW of co-creation. Superpower 1 outlines the challenges for an individual participant of a co-creative process and offers insights and shortcuts to overcome

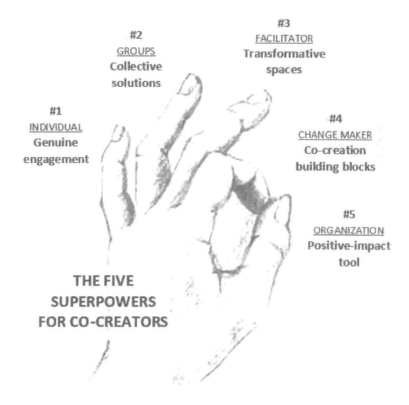

Figure 10.1 The Five Superpowers for Co-creators

some of the toughest challenges we have encountered in our work. Super-power 2 describes challenges at the team and group level and offers insights in how to advance processes when group-related conflicts or tensions prevent a smooth progress. The different elements described show how to associate tensions back to underlying strengths, allowing to find back to a level of understanding and empathy that is needed when different interest groups meet. Superpower 3 considers the overarching space of collaboration that typically a facilitator is expected to hold for the involved stakeholders. This is the most subtle and most sensitive superpower and if you have a sensitivity for the energy in a room and among people, you'll find yourself a natural here. It is to least talked about and the possibly most important of all superpowers. The ability to create and hold a space for stakeholders to go through the various phases of a messy co-creation, navigating through all kinds of storms, crevasses, peaks and lows. This is the space of the true adventurer – a gifted facilitator is a magician. A person equipped with endless tricks and tools that are used always in the right moment to enable the right next experience and aha to occur.

Superpowers 4 and 5 are two different approaches to tame the different steps of co-creation – different phases of co-creation that together build a cohesive whole. These superpowers are about the WHAT of co-creation. Superpower 4 provides an overview of the ideal steps that when put together provide a comprehensive and complete succession of activities leading to a concrete desired outcome for the project at hand. Not every project needs all steps and this superpower is an enabler for the initiator, often a change-maker, who is about to take on a burning issue with the desire to get the right people together to solve it. If you feel you have a good feeling for process steps, you may be far along in sensing how to build a process for success. Superpower 5 is specially designed for the many heroes in corporations, those change agents that work inside smaller or larger organizations and that know that they can make a true difference at their place of work. They also know that corporations are special animals with a limited attention span and a great need for high efficiency and effectiveness. If a team spends a day together on a new project, it is better produces a useable output. So superpower 5 is for those who need a clear-cut, pragmatic and adaptable process that can with-stand the demands and scrutiny of a CFO and CEO. The SDGXCHANGE process is one such well-tested answer. If you are a corporate strategist or in charge of corporate innovation, or have a great strategic or innovative mind, you will find this superpower offering you insights to further augment what you may have experienced, used and learned. It may be just what you need to feel that wind underneath your wings so that you can take off and transform your organization into a force for good.

There is an additional important chapter that talks about the various types of change makers. It aims at enlarging our horizon so that we think beyond the classical person who would typically lead such a co-creation process.

While there is of course there is nothing more important the person itself that will trigger, lead or contribute to the process, I didn't feel comfortable naming this a superpower. I chose HOW and WHAT aspects of co-creation rather than different personality options when I defined superpowers.

And finally, of course, there are the two introductory chapters in Part 1 that set the stage for the discussion in the book. There is a bit of magic in there when we look at the shift between the stage of competition to the stage of collaboration and I think my friend Robert Quinn for this insight. This shift as well as the mutual dependency of society and business are fundamental realities on which the co-creation process builds. Understanding them helps better framing a co-creation project, while it doesn't take this actual knowledge to explore the superpowers that the books explores.

I truly hope that you find affinity and support to develop and unleash your own superpower, may it be one distinct power among the five I suggest, or may it be your own magic cocktail of knowledge, skills and attitudes that equip you with competencies so unique and so superior that when you are in the room with everything you have, that you can contribute to create that magic that is needed to realize the ambitious projects we need to realize to move towards the save space our civilization needs to reach, so that we can all live well on this one planet we call mother Earth.

Feel free to reach out to me on LinkedIn, on www.collaboratory2030.org or katrinmuff.com or contacting my email. I am just like you – wishing to make a difference and seeking a way to contribute. I know that together, we can and will succeed and you can count on my support if there is anything I can do to help you and your project succeed!

Bibliography

Business Sustainability Today website: https://sustainability-today.com/ accessed March 21, 2018.

Bushe, Gervase R., & Marshak, Robert J. (2015): The dialogic mindset in organization development. The dialogic mindset in organization development. *Research in Organizational Change and Development* Vol 22, 55–97.

Bouwen, R., & Taillieu, T. (2004): Multi-party collaboration as social learning for interdependence: Developing relational knowing for sustainable natural resource management. *Journal of Community & Applied Social Psychology* Vol 14 No 3, 137–153.

Cameron, Kim S., Quinn, Robert E., DeGraff, Jeff, & Thakor, AnJannick V. (2006): *Competing values leadership: Creating value in organizations*. Edward Elgar Publishing Limited, Cheltenham.

Competency Assessment for Responsible Leadership (CARL): https://carl2030.org/ accessed March 18, 2018.

Confino, J. (2012): Unilever's Paul Polman: Challenging the corporate status quo. *The Guardian*, April 24: www.theguardian.com/sustainable-business/paul-polman-unilever-sustainable-living-plan accessed March 28, 2018.

Dialogic Organizational Developmental: www.dialogicod.net accessed November 21, 2017.

Dyllick, Thomas, & Muff, Katrin (2014): Students leading collaboratories. In: *The Collaboratory – a co-creative stakeholder engagement process for solving complex issues*. Muff, K. (ed.). Greenleaf Publishing, Sheffield, pp. 127–133.

Dyllick, Thomas, & Muff, Katrin (2016): What does sustainability for business really mean? And when is a business truly sustainable? In: *Sustainable business: A one planet approach*. Jeanrenaud, S., Gosling, J., & Jeanrenaud, J.P. (eds.). Wiley, Chichester, pp. 381–407.

Dyllick, Thomas, & Rost, Zoe (2017): Towards true product sustainability. *Journal of Cleaner Production* Vol 162, 346–360.

Focused Reporting: www.focusedreporting.ch/ accessed March 16, 2018.

Gapframe – a translator of the SDGs into national priorities for business and change makers: www.gapframe.org accessed March 30, 2018.

Gardner, Howard (1997): *Extraordinary minds – portraits of four exceptional individuals and an examination of our own extraordinariness*. Basic book, New York.

Goldman Schuyler, Kathryn, Skjei, Susan, Sanzgiri, Jyotsna, & Koskela, Virpi (2016): Moments of waking up: A doorway to mindfulness and presence. *Journal of Management Inquiry*, 1–15.

Goleman, Daniel (1998): *Working with emotional intelligence*. Bantam, New York.

Graves, C.W. (1970): Levels of existence: An open system theory of values. *Journal of Humanistic Psychology* Vol 10 No 2, 131–155.

HeartMath: www.heartmath.com/ accessed March 30, 2018.

Impact Leadership Program: www.bsl-lausanne.ch/program/executive-and-continuing-education/impact-leadership-program/

Hillman, Os (2011): *Change agent: Engaging your passion to be the one who makes a difference.* Charisma House, Lake Mary.

Huh, Yeol, Reigeluth, Charles M., & Lee, Dabae (2014): Collective efficacy and its relationship with leadership in a computer-mediated project-based group work. *Contemporary Educational Technology* Vol 1 No 5, 1–21.

Kahane, Adam (2010): *Power and Love – a theory and practice of social change.* Berret-Koehler Publishing, San Francisco.

Muff, Katrin (ed.) (2014): *The Collaboratory – a co-creative stakeholder engagement process for solving complex issues.* Greenleaf Publishing, Sheffield.

Muff, Katrin (2014): Designing a Collaboratory: A narrative roadmap. In: *The Collaboratory – a co-creative stakeholder engagement process for solving complex issues.* Muff, K. (ed.). Greenleaf Publishing, Sheffield, pp. 229–245.

Muff, Katrin (2017): How the circle model can purpose-orient entrepreneurial universities. *Journal of Management Development – Special Issue Entrepreneurial University*, Vol 36 No 2, 146–162.

Muff, Katrin: *Leadership Competencies Survey.* Unpublished data accessible on request through katrin.muff@gmail.com

Muff, Katrin, Kapalka, Agnieszka, & Dyllick, Thomas (2017): The Gap Frame – Translating the SDGs into relevant national grand challenges for strategic business opportunities. *International Journal of Management Education* Vol 15, 363–383.

Muff, Katrin, Liechti Anna, & Dyllick, Thomas (2018): The Competency Assessment for Responsible Leadership (CARL) – consolidating the responsible leadership discourse into an online tool. *Journal of Business Ethics* (in review process). Article accessible via katrin.muff@gmail.com until publication

Price-Mitchell, Marilyn (2015): *Tomorrow's change makers: Reclaiming the power of citizenship for a new generation.* Eagle Harbor Publishing, Bainbridge Island.

Quinn, Robert E. (2004): *Building the bridge as you walk on it.* Jossey Bass, San Francisco.

RepRisk: www.reprisk.com/ accessed March 16, 2018.

Scharmer, Otto Scharmer (2015): The Blindspot: www.huffingtonpost.com/otto-scharmer/uncovering-the-grammar-of-the-social-field_b_7524910.html

Schamer, Otto Scharmer (2016): *Theory U: Leading from the future as it emerges.* Second edition. Berret-Koehler Publishing, San Francisco.

SDGXCHANGE and the SDGX innovation process: www.sdgx.org accessed March 16, 2018; Organizational Culture Assessment Instrument (OCAI): www.ocai-online.com/ accessed March 16, 2018.

Smit, Arnold: About CARL. *Soundcloud*: https://soundcloud.com/business-school-lausanne/interview-with-dr-arnold-smit-by-tony-johnston accessed March 18, 2018.

Sustainable Development Goals (SDGs) by the United Nations (2015): www.un.org/sustainabledevelopment/blog/2015/09/why-should-you-care-about-the-sustainable-development-goals/ accessed March 30, 2018.

Thompson, Laurie Ann (2014): *Be a changemaker: How to start something that matters.* Simon Pulse/Beyond Words, Hillsboro.

United Nations Global Compact: www.unglobalcompact.org accessed March 30, 2018.

United Nations: The Sustainable Development Goals (SDGs): www.un.org/sustainabledeve lopment accessed March 30, 2018.

Vermeesch, Inge, Art, Dewulf, Marc, Craps, & Katrien, Termeer (2013): A relational perspective on leadership in multi-actor governance networks for sustainable materials management. *Towards a Framework Based on Complexity Leadership Paper Presented at the 1st International Conference on Public Policy Grenoble* June 26–28, 2013 http://archives.ippa publicpolicy.org/IMG/pdf/panel_43_s1_vermeesch.pdf last accessed July 29, 2018.

Watkins, Alan, & Wilber, Ken (2015): *Wicked and wise – how to solve the world's toughest problems.* Urban Publishing, Croydon.

Wilson, David S. (2007): Rethinking the theoretical foundation of sociobiology. *The Quarterly Review of Biology* Vol 82 No 4, 327–348.

World Business Council for Sustainable Business: Reporting matters: www.wbcsd.org/ Projects/Reporting/Reporting-matters accessed March 16, 2018.

World Business Council for Sustainable Development: www.wbcsd.org accessed March 30, 2018.

World Economic Forum: www.weforum.org accessed March 30, 2018.

Index